MW01285678

Elite • 138

The Yugoslav Wars (1)

Slovenia & Croatia 1991–95

Dr N Thomas & K Mikulan • Illustrated by D Pavlovic

Consultant editor Martin Windrow

First published in Great Britain in 2006 by Osprey Publishing,
Midland House, West Way, Botley, Oxford OX2 0PH, UK
443 Park Avenue South, New York, NY 10016, USA
Email: info@ospreypublishing.com

ISBN 1 84176 963 0

Editor: Martin Windrow
Page layouts by Ken Vail Graphic Design, Cambridge, UK (kvgd.com)
Maps by Darko Pavlovic
Index by Glyn Sutcliffe
Originated by The Electronic Page Company, UK
Printed in China through World Print Ltd.

06 07 08 09 10   10 9 8 7 6 5 4 3 2 1

A CIP catalog record for this book is available from the British Library

FOR A CATALOGUE OF ALL BOOKS PUBLISHED BY
OSPREY MILITARY AND AVIATION PLEASE CONTACT:

North America:
Osprey Direct
C/o Random House Distribution Center, 400 Hahn Road,
Westminster, MD 21157, USA
Email: info@ospreydirect.com

All other regions:
Osprey Direct UK
PO Box 140, Wellingborough, Northants, NN8 2FA, UK
Email: info@ospreydirect.co.uk

Buy online at www.ospreypublishing.com

Acknowledgements

Nigel Thomas would like to thank Seph Nesbit and Janez J.
Svajncer; also his wife Heather and their sons Alexander
and especially Dominick for their encouragement and
support. Krunoslav Mikulan would like to thank Tihomir
Bregar, Henrik Clausen, Col Ivica Olujic, Sinisa Pogacic,
Borivoj Radojcic, Emil Smutni, WO Class I Damir Srebric
and Maj Ante Simatovic; also his wife Rolanda and their son
Bruno, to whom he is deeply indebted for help and support
during the time he spent researching.

Artist's Note

Readers may care to note that the original paintings from
which the colour plates in this book were prepared are
available for private sale. All reproduction copyright
whatsoever is retained by the Publishers. All enquiries
should be addressed to:

Darko Pavlovic, Modecova 3, Zagreb, 10090, Croatia

The Publishers regret that they can enter into no
correspondence upon this matter.

GLOSSARY OF MILITARY & NATIONAL ACRONYMS

ATJ	Croatian Police Counter-Terrorist Unit
ATVP	Croatian Military Police Counter-Terrorist Units
HOS	Croatian paramilitary organization
HRM	Croatian Navy (1991 >)
HV	Croatian Army (Sept 1991 >)
JNA	Yugoslav People's Army
JRM	Yugoslav Navy
MUP	Croatian Ministry of Interior (commanding Police)
NDH	Independent State of Croatia (1941–45)
NZ	Croatian People's Defence Force (1991–92)
PEM	Slovene Special Police
PP	Croatian Judicial Police
PSTO	Slovene Military Districts
RSK	Republic of Serbian Krajina (Dec 1991 >)
SAOs	Serbian Autonomous Regions in Croatia
SCP	Croatian-Serb paramilitary group
SDG	Croatian-Serb paramilitary group
SEM	Slovene Counter-Terrorist Police
SG	Croatian-Serb paramilitary group
SHS	Kingdom of Serbs, Croats & Slovenes (1918–29)
SJM	Krajina Special Police
SJP	Croatian Special Police Units
SRJ	Socialist Republic of Yugoslavia (Serbia & Montenegro, April 1992 >)
SV	Slovene Army (Aug 1995 >)
SVRSK, SVK	Serbian Army of Krajina (Oct 1992 >)
TO	Territorial Defence Forces of the Yugoslav republics
VJ	Yugoslav Army (May 1992 >)
VRS	Bosnian-Serb Army (May 1992 >)
ZNG	Croatian National Guard Corps (1991 >)

THE YUGOSLAV WARS (1)
SLOVENIA & CROATIA 1991–95

THE POLITICAL CONTEXT

On 1 December 1918 Serbia (including Macedonia) and Montenegro – states which had fought with the victorious Allies in World War I – united with the 'State of the Slovenes, Croats and Serbs', formed on 29 October 1918 from the Slovene, Croatian and Bosnia-Herzegovinian provinces of the defeated Austro-Hungarian Empire. This entity was named the Kingdom of the Serbs, Croats and Slovenes (SHS). On 6 January 1929 the kingdom was renamed Yugoslavia ('Land of the South Slavs'). On 2 December 1945 the kingdom was replaced by a Federative People's (from 1963, Socialist Federative) Republic of Yugoslavia. On 27 April 1992 the republic was reconstituted with Serbia and Montenegro only, and on 4 February 2003 this rump state was renamed 'Serbia and Montenegro'.

JNA conscripts parade in 1990, wearing the *titovka* sidecap, M77 winter coat, and leather belt with two shoulder braces; they present arms with the M70 automatic rifle, a Yugoslav copy of the ubiquitous AK-47 Kalashnikov. (Nigel Thomas Collection)

The historical background

Throughout the 15th–19th centuries these Balkan provinces of the Ottoman Turkish Empire comprised a large number of Slav and non-Slav nationalities, including minorities scattered chaotically among majorities in enclaves and mixed borderlands. The Serbs, at about 40 per cent of the total population the largest nationality, were followed by the Croats (25 per cent), Slovenes (9 per cent), Macedonians (5 per cent), Bosnian Moslems (5 per cent), Albanians (4 per cent), Hungarians (3 per cent) and Montenegrins (3 per cent); there were also much smaller minorities of Czechs, Slovaks, Bulgarians, Italians, Germans, Vlachs, Turks, Gypsies, Romanians and others. The political rivalry between the two largest nationalities – the Serbs and Croats – caused most of the instability that haunted the Yugoslav state during its 73-year history from 1918 to 1992.

From long before 1918 many Serbs believed that they would only be secure if united in a single Serbian state. This goal was effectively achieved in 1918, when the Serbs were convinced that Serbia's record in World War I, and their status as the largest nationality, entitled them to a leadership rôle in the new SHS. Serbian nationalists supported a centralized state united around the Serbian monarchy and the Orthodox church. However, most Croats – historically Roman Catholics – had assumed that the new kingdom would be a federal state with no dominant nationality. They were therefore horrified when the regent, Prince Aleksandar, in the St Vitus Day Constitution of 28 June 1921, abolished traditional Croatian institutions and introduced a centralized state led by a Serbian nationalist, Nikola Pasic. Resulting tensions boiled over on 20 June 1928 with the assassination of the Croatian leader Stjepan Radic. Aleksandar proclaimed a royal dictatorship on 6 January 1929, abolishing political parties and appointing a government with the Royal Guard commander, Gen Petar Zivkovic, as prime minister. The king renamed the state 'Yugoslavia', further frustrating Croatian hopes of a federal state.

Thereafter the Serbian-dominated police and gendarmerie suppressed Croatian and Slovene political opposition, prompting the Croatian Party of Rights parliamentarian Ante Pavelic to form his extreme right wing Ustasha Movement. Fleeing into exile, he and Macedonian VMRO nationalists organized the assassination of King Aleksandar in Marseilles on 9 October 1934. Intensified political repression followed until Radic's successor, Vladko Macek, largely restored Serbian-Croatian relations by negotiating with the regent, Prince Pavle, to secure limited Croatian political autonomy on 20 August 1939.

Although Serbia was traditionally drawn towards Great Britain and France, her World War I allies, Pavle pursued a tactical policy of friendship with Nazi Germany and Fascist Italy. However, his signing of a Tripartite Pact with Hitler and Mussolini on 25 March 1941 provoked the Serbian-dominated Yugoslav armed forces to depose the regent two days later, in favour of the 18-year-old King Petar II. Hitler immediately ordered the invasion of Yugoslavia; on 6 April Axis forces invaded, forcing the internally divided Royal Yugoslav Army to surrender on 17 April. This spelled the end of 'Old Yugoslavia'.

The Tito years

Hitler dismembered Yugoslavia, allowing Pavelic's Ustashas to form an Independent State of Croatia (NDH), comprising most of Croatia and Bosnia-Herzegovina; and establishing a client state from the rump of Serbia. Slovenia, Macedonia, Montenegro, Vojvodina, Kosovo and the Croatian coast were divided between Germany, Italy, Italian-annexed Albania, Hungary and Bulgaria.

Pavelic ordered his Ustasha army to murder, deport or forcibly convert to Roman Catholicism the 1.8 million Serb minority in Croatia, realizing the worst fears of Serbian nationalists, and provoking the first Serbian/Croatian armed conflict in history. Meanwhile, in April 1941 Col Dragoljub 'Draza' Mihailovic formed the 'Chetnik' guerrilla movement in Serbia, while Josip Broz 'Tito' established in July the rival communist 'Partisans', and both declared war against Axis occupation forces and the NDH. Tito recruited from all nationalities and promised

Yugoslav Minister of Defence *General-pukovnik* Veljko Kadijevic (far right) and President Janez Drnovsek (centre) inspecting a JNA unit, 1989. The officers are wearing the *titovka* and the M77 winter coat; the officer (far left) has the tank crews' fur-collared winter coat. (Nigel Thomas Collection)

a federal Yugoslavia, while Mihailovic, drawing most of his support from Serbs, hoped to re-establish pre-war centralist Yugoslavia. By May 1942 some Chetniks had begun local co-operation with Axis forces against the Partisans; in November 1943 the Allies decided to back the Partisans, and in May 1944 abandoned Mihailovic. When Germany and the NDH surrendered on 8 May 1945, Tito's Yugoslav Army had occupied all of Yugoslavia, exacting a murderous revenge on thousands of Slovene, NDH and Chetnik troops who had fought with the Germans.

On 2 December 1945 Tito proclaimed the Federative People's Republic of Yugoslavia as a one-party state comprising six republics and provinces: Bosnia-Herzegovina, Croatia, Macedonia, Montenegro, Serbia (including the Kosovo-Metohija and Vojvodina Autonomous Provinces) and Slovenia. Although a communist, Tito pursued a skilful foreign policy independent of the Soviet Union; after 1948 he developed links with Western Europe, also achieving reconciliation with the USSR in 1955, and by 1960 he was regarded as a leader of the 'non-aligned' group of states. On 7 April 1963 the country was renamed the Socialist Federative Republic of Yugoslavia (SFRJ).

Tito's political cunning, pragmatism and personal charisma, backed by his ruthless UDBa security apparatus, brought more than two decades of relative economic prosperity to Yugoslavia, and an uneasy stability between her restive nationalities. Nevertheless, the more economically productive republics of Slovenia and Croatia and Vojvodina Province increasingly resented the cost of subsidizing the poorer regions.

The collapse of Yugoslavia, 1991

On 21 February 1974 a new constitution was adopted, intended to preserve stability and union by devolving many powers, including police and some defence, to the republics and autonomous provinces. On 4 May 1980 the 88-year-old President Tito died, and power was duly transferred to an eight-man presidency drawn from the republics and provinces, with the position of Federal President rotating annually.

JNA infantry wearing snow-camouflage hooded smocks and trousers over M77 field uniforms; the M53 machine gun is a Yugoslav copy of the German MG42. (Nigel Thomas Collection)

However, this idealistic arrangement proved inherently impractical.

On 24 September 1986 the Serbian Academy of Sciences circulated an anonymous memorandum claiming that Serbs in Kosovo province were being persecuted by the Albanian majority, and that Serbs in Croatia were dangerously exposed to resurgent Croatian nationalists. In spring 1987 Slobodan Milosevic, President of the Serbian Communist Party, saw an opportunity to further his political ambitions by creating – even if he could not retain Yugoslavia's existing borders – a new Serbian-dominated Yugoslavia: even if he lost Slovenia, Croatia and Macedonia, he hoped to retain key Croatian districts by expelling the Croat minorities and populating them with Croatian-Serbs[1], and taking over most of Bosnia-Herzegovina. Similarly, he planned to restore a Serbian majority in Kosovo by expelling Kosovar Albanians; and on 28 March 1989 he revoked Kosovan and Vojvodinan autonomy, asserting direct Serbian control over these provinces. As Milosevic, elected President of Serbia in May 1989, consolidated his power in Serbia, Montenegro, Vojvodina and Kosovo, he misrepresented Slovene and Croatian ambitions for greater decentralization and democracy as an intention to secede from Yugoslavia. Both Slovenia and Croatia held multi-party elections; on 8 April 1990 Milan Kucan, leader of the social democratic Demos party, was elected as the first non-communist President of Slovenia, and on 30 May Franjo Tudjman, leader of the nationalist HDZ party, became President of Croatia.

Relations between on the one hand Serbia and Montenegro, dominated by Milosevic, and Slovenia and Croatia on the other, deteriorated rapidly. On 23 December 1990 Slovenia voted for complete independence from Yugoslavia. On 28 February 1991 the Serbian National Council, representing the Serbian minority in Croatia, declared its independence from Croatia and continued adherence to Milosevic's Yugoslavia. On 16 March 1991 Milosevic declared that Serbia would no longer obey federal directives and that 'Yugoslavia is finished'. Finally, on 25 June 1991, Slovenia and Croatia formally declared their independence, and two days later units of the federal Yugoslav People's Army (JNA) in Slovenia and Croatia were mobilized against the secessionist states.

---

[1] In this text, minorities are described by this order of words, e.g. Croatian-Serbs are ethnic Serbs living within the historic borders of Croatia.

THE YUGOSLAV PEOPLE'S ARMY

The army formed on 1 Mar 1945 from Tito's Partisan units was redesignated the Yugoslav People's Army (*Jugoslovenska Narodna Armija* – JNA) on 22 Dec 1951, to underline its communist identity. It comprised all land, naval and air forces. In Sept 1968 the formation of the Territorial Defence Force (TO) was authorized, to support the JNA. On 21 Feb 1974, TO brigades were subordinated to their respective republics or provinces, and the JNA and TO were regarded as equal components of the Yugoslav Armed Forces (*Oruzane Snage* SFRJ).

As the political situation deteriorated during the 1980s tension arose between the JNA and TO, and the central government became concerned that the latter might be used by republican leaders to secede from Yugoslavia; consequently, in spring 1981 the 130,000-strong Kosovo TO was disarmed to prevent Kosovar-Albanians gaining access to weapons, and in 1988 the JNA absorbed the entire TO. On 29 Sept 1989, Gen Blagoje Adzic became chief of the armed forces general staff; he was a Bosnian Serb, and his family's murder by Ustasha troops in late 1941 had made him deeply suspicious of Croatian nationalism.

Under the 1974 constitution the Land Forces (*Kopnena vojska* – KoV) were divided into six field armies allocated to the five republics: 1 Army (HQ Belgrade) – northern Serbia and Vojvodina; 2 Army (Nis) – southern Serbia and Kosovo; 3 Army (Skopje) – Macedonia; 5 Army (Zagreb) – Croatia; 7 Army (Sarajevo) – Bosnia-Herzegovina; 9 Army (Ljubljana); plus 2 Corps (Titograd) – Montenegro, and also some elements in the Coastal Naval District (Split), formerly 4 Army. In 1988 these Armies were

JNA *Desetar* (left – for listing of ranks, see page 57), in summer field uniform, wearing the M59/85 helmet with a painted red star badge just visible, and the M75 summer shirt. He instructs a female member of the Territorial Defence Force (TO), who carries an obsolete Kragujevac Mauser M48 bolt-action rifle, a copy of the German Karabiner 98k. (Nigel Thomas Collection)

reorganized into Military Districts no longer corresponding to republican borders, thereby making it more difficult for republics to control their own units. Infantry divisions were reorganized into corps, apart from the élite corps-sized Proletarian Guards Mechanized Division. By June 1991 the land forces comprised about 165,600 men (40,000 officers, 125,600 NCOs and men) organized as follows:

1 Military District (Belgrade) – Northern Theatre Northern Serbia, NE Croatia (Slavonia), Bosnia-Herzegovina and Vojvodina. This had 90,000 troops in the Belgrade Defence Command, six corps (4, 5, 12, 17, 24 & 37), the Bosnia-Herzegovinian TO, and parts of the Serbian and Croatian TOs.

3 Military District (Skopje) – South-Eastern Theatre Southern Serbia, Kosovo, inland Montenegro and Macedonia. 60,000 troops in five weak corps (2, 21, 41, 42 & 52), the Macedonian TO, and parts of the Serbian and Montenegrin TOs.

5 Military District (Zagreb) – North-Western Theatre Slovenia and W Croatia. 90,000 men in five corps (10, 13, 14, 31 & 32), the Slovenian TO and part of the Croatian TO.

Naval Military District (Split) SE Croatia (Dalmatia) and the Croatian and Montenegrin coastline, comprising three naval sectors and controlling the Yugoslav Navy and naval infantry; 20,000 men in 9 Corps and two brigades, and parts of the Croatian and Montenegrin TOs.

No complete official JNA order of battle has been published, but the accompanying Table 1 represents the units known to have existed in July 1991. 'Guards' units were based in Belgrade to protect the government, while the term 'Proletarian', first used in World War II, designated élite units.

Two formidable-looking officers of the JNA's crack 63 Parachute Bde, displaying the brown M70 paratrooper beret with officer's cap badge – a white and gold parachute on a blue background, beneath a red star edged gold, in a silver wreath. They wear the standard camouflage jacket with two D-rings mounted on each breast; the right-hand man shows the rank patch of a *Major* on his left breast. This unit failed to live up to its reputation during the 'Ten-Day War' against Slovenian secessionist forces. (Nigel Thomas Collection)

Table 1: Battle Order of Yugoslav People's Army, June 1991 (partial)

GHQ (Belgrade)

1 Prol Gds Mech Div (1, 2 & 3 Gds Mech Bdes); 63 Para Bde, 138 Transport Air Bde

1 MILITARY DISTRICT (Belgrade)

152 Mix Arty Bde, 1 Mix AT Bde

Belgrade Defence Command 151 Mot Bde, 22 Mix Arty Rgt, 22 AT Rgt

4 Corps (Sarajevo) 6, 10, 49 & 651 Mot Bdes; 7, 216 & Romanija Mtn Bdes; 120 Lt Inf Bde; *reserve*, 13 Ptsn Div. *S&S:* 4 Mix Arty Rgt, 4 Mix AT Rgt, 240 Mob AA Miss Rgt, 346 Lt AA Rgt, 340 Eng Rgt, 4 Eng Bn, 367 Sig Rgt, 4 Sig Bn, 593 NBC Rgt, 4 MP Bn

5 Corps (Banja Luka) 329 Armd Bde; 16, 327 & 343 Mot Bdes; 122 & 149 Lt Inf Bdes; 5 Mix Arty Bde, 5 Mix AT Bde; *reserve*, 10 Ptsn Div, 30 Ptsn Div (6, 11, 18 & 19 Ptsn Bdes). *S&S:* 5 Lt AA Rgt, 293 Eng Rgt, 188 Pon Bn, 5 Sig Bn, 5 MP Bn

12 Corps (Novi Sad) 505 Armd Bde; 36, 51 & 453 Mech Bdes; 506 Inf Bde; *reserve*, 20 Ptsn Div

17 Corps (Tuzla) 12 Prol Mech Bde; 91, 336 & 395 Mot Bdes; 17 & 192 Lt Inf Bdes; 158 Mix AT Bde; *reserve*, ? Ptsn Div (17 & 22 Ptsn Bdes). *S&S:* ? Mix Arty Rgt, 17 Lt AA Rgt, 17 Mix AT Rgt, 497 Eng Rgt, 17 Pon Bn, 17 Sig Bn, 17 MP Bn

24 Corps (Kragujevac) 252 Armd Bde

37 Corps (Titovo Uzice) 326 Armd Bde; 5, 145 & 437 Mot Bdes; 6, 19 & 215 Mtn Bdes. *S&S:* 31 & 208 Arty Rgts, 417 Mix AT Rgt, 37 MP Bn

1 Air & AA Corps

3 MILITARY DISTRICT (Skopje)

150 Mix Arty Bde, 101 Mix AT Bde

2 Corps (Titograd)

21 Corps (Nis) 211 Armd Bde

41 Corps (Bitola) 243 Prol Armd Bde

42 Corps (Kumanovo) 592 Mot Bde

52 Corps (Pristina) 15 Prol Mech Bde, 125 Mot Bde

3 Air & AA Corps

5 MILITARY DISTRICT (Zagreb)

Mix Artillery Bde, NBC Rgt, Pon Bn, Border Guard units, helicopter sqn

10 Corps (Zagreb) 4 Armd Bde: 31 & 140 Mech Bde; 8 Prol, 257 & 622 Mot Bdes; 6 & 580 Mix Arty Bdes, 6 Mix AT Bde; *reserve*, 33 Ptsn Div. *S&S:* 149 Mob AA & 155 AA Miss Rgts, 151 Lt AA Bn, 123 & 671 Pon Bns, 258 Eng Rgt, 10 Eng Bn, 10 Sig Bn, 10 Auto Bn, 10 MP Bn

Krajina TO units (Kordun & Lika) 1, 2, 4, 7 Ptsn, 11 & 145 Lt Bdes

13 Corps (Rijeka) 13 & 236 Prol Mot Bdes; 6 Mtn Bde; *reserve*, 35 Ptsn Div (2x bdes + mortar bn), 43 Ptsn Div (3x bdes + mtr bn). *S&S:* 13 Mix Arty Rgt, 13 Lt AA Rgt, 13 Mix AT Rgt, 127 Eng Rgt, 540 Pon Bn, 13 Sig Bn, 13 NBC Bn, 13 Auto Bn, 13 MP Bn, 13 Recce Co, 13 Repl Bn, 13 Med Bn

14 Corps (Ljubljana) 1 Armd Bde; 228 Mot Bde; 269 Mtn Bde. *S&S:* ? Mix Arty Rgt, ? Lt AA Rgt, detached AT Co, ? Eng Rgt, ? Mix AT Rgt, 14 Sig Bn, 14 Cdo Det, 289 MP Bn

31 Corps (Maribor) 145, 195 & 325 Mot Bdes; *reserve*, 29 Ptsn Div. *S&S:* ? Mix Arty Rgt, ? Lt AA Rgt, 417 Mix AT Rgt, 2x detached AT Cos, ? Eng Rgt, 31 Sig Bn, ? Cdo Det, 31 MP Bn

32 Corps (Varazdin) 32 Mech Bde; 265 Armd Bde; 288 Mix AT Bde. *S&S:* ? Arty Rgt, Eng Rgt, 32 Sig Bn, 32 MP Bn

5 Air & AA Corps

NAVAL MILITARY DISTRICT (Split)

9 Corps (Knin) 1, (+ later 11), 180 & 221 Mot Bdes; *reserve*, 1 Ptsn Bde. *S&S:* 9 Mix Arty Rgt, 271 Lt AA Rgt, 557 Mix AT Rgt, 594 Eng Rgt, 70 Sig Bn, 9 MP Bn; **plus 3x bdes Krajina TO**

5 Naval Sector (Pula) 5 Mot Bde; **8 Nav Sect (Split)** 12 Amphib Bde; **9 Nav Sect (Kumbor)** 24 Mot Bde

(**Key:** ? – unit unidentified, AA – Anti-aircraft, AT = Anti-tank, Arty = Artillery, Auto = Automobile, Cdo = Commando, Det = Detachment, Gds = Guards, MP = Military Police, Mech = Mechanized, Med = Medical, Miss = Missile, Mix = Mixed, Mob = Mobile, Mot = Motorized, Mtn = Mountain, Pon = Pontoon, Ptsn = Partisan, Prol = Proletarian, Repl = Replacement; S&S = corps support & service assets)

There were then 17 numbered and named corps: five Serbian (12, 21, 24, 37 & 52); one Montenegrin (2); two Slovene (14 & 31); four Croatian (9, 10, 13 & 32); three Bosnia-Herzegovinian (4, 5 & 17); and two Macedonian (41 & 42). Each Theatre had 5–6 corps plus Military District HQ troops, usually comprising at least a mixed artillery brigade and mixed anti-tank brigade. A corps had Corps HQ troops with three regiments (mixed artillery, mixed AT, light AA artillery), and six battalions (engineers, signals, military police, NBC, medical and replacement); and about four armoured, mechanized and motorized brigades, supported by infantry, light infantry and mountain brigades. During operations in Slovenia and Croatia the corps and brigade organization was modified, combat brigades in the N & NW Theatres being reinforced with extra units from the SE Theatre; battalions were often upgraded to regiments and regiments to brigades, while some units were disbanded when a majority of their Slovene and Croatian personnel deserted.

Reserve units were organized into nine identified Partisan Divs (10, 13, 20, 28, 29, 30, 33, 35 & 43), each containing a number of Partisan Bdes, of which 22 (1, 3–7, 11, 13, 17–22, 24, 27, 33, 35, 36, 46, 63 & 81) have been identified.

Seventy-one brigades can be confirmed: nine armoured (1, 4, 211, 243 Proletarian, 252, 265, 326, 329 & 505); 11 mechanized (1–3, 12 & 15 Prol, 31, 32, 36, 51, 140 & 453); 29 motorized (1, 5, 6, 8 Prol, 10, 11, 13

Two JNA Military Policemen wearing rust-brown berets, camouflage jackets with a national flag patch on the left upper sleeve, and the white belts and M63 buckles sported by MPs. (Henrik Clausen)

Prol, 16, 23, 24, 49, 92, 125, 145, 151, 180, 195, 221, 228, 236 Prol, 257, 325, 327, 336, 343, 395, 437, 592 & 622); one infantry (506); five light infantry (17, 120, 122, 149 & 192); six mountain (6, 7, 19, 215, 216 & 269); four mixed artillery (6, 150, 52 & 580); and six mixed AT (1, 5, 6, 102, 158 & 288).

An armoured brigade comprised three armoured battalions, each battalion having 31 M-84 or T-55 tanks divided between three ten-tank companies. A mechanized brigade had 2–3 mechanized battalions with Soviet BRDM-2 scout cars and M-980 or BVP-M-80A infantry carriers; and 1–2 armoured battalions. A motorized brigade had 2–3 motorized battalions (each with three infantry companies) with M-60P APCs, and 1–2 armoured battalions.

The **Yugoslav Navy** (*Ratna mornarica* – RM) totalled about 10,000 officers and men: 6,800 in the frigates, corvettes, submarines, missile, torpedo and patrol boats of the Adriatic Fleet and River Flotilla; 2,300 manning 25 coastal artillery batteries; and 900 light infantry in 12 Amphibious Brigade. Following Soviet practice the **Yugoslav Air Force** was designated Air Force & Anti-Aircraft Artillery (*Ratno vazduhoplovstvo i protivvazdusna odbrana* – RV i PVO), with headquarters at Zemun near Belgrade. There were about 360 combat and 440 non-combat aircraft divided between three air corps (1, 3 & 5) and attached to the correspondingly numbered military districts. The air component had 28 fixed-wing and 11 helicopter squadrons grouped into six brigades – five air (82, 97, 98, 111 & 119) and one transport (138) – each with 3–5 squadrons; and seven regiments – three fighter (83, 117 & 204), three fighter-bomber (105, 172 & 185) and one helicopter (107) – with 2–3 squadrons. The AA Artillery comprised one surface-to-air missile brigade and two regiments.

The **Territorial Defence Force** (*Teritorijalna odbrana* – TO), with a paper strength of 1.5 million, formed a second line of defence and was intended to harass Soviet forces who penetrated into the Yugoslav hinterland. On 21 Feb 1974, TO units were subordinated to republican headquarters (RSTO), reporting to the presidents of the eight republics and provinces; and in 1978 TO brigades were grouped into TO divisions. However, in 1987 the JNA reasserted itself, and in 1988 the RSTOs were subordinated to the local Military District. On 14 May 1990 the JNA took over the Slovene, Croatian and Bosnia-Herzegovinian TO armouries, and confiscated all weapons not held by Croatian-Serb and Bosnian-Serb units. By 27 June 1991 only Serbs and Montenegrins could be trusted to report for duty. Consequently only nine Serbian TO divisions (including 10, 13, 20, 29, 30, 33, 35 & 43) were confirmed as contributing to the JNA war-effort, operating as light infantry equipped with obsolete small arms.

* * *

The JNA had enjoyed an international reputation as a powerful, well-equipped and well-trained force, but the political crises of the 1980s degraded its efficiency. Traditionally the JNA had been multi-ethnic, though with Serbs and Montenegrins overrepresented among the officer corps, and Croats dominating the Navy. By 1990, however, as Slovene and Croatian secession became more likely, almost all Slovenes, Croats and Bosnian-Croats (and also many Bosnian-Moslems, Kosovar-Albanians, Vojvodina-Hungarians and Macedonians) were unwilling to serve in an army which might soon be fighting their fellow-countrymen. The impact of this is exemplified by 5 Military District, which bore the brunt of the fighting in 1991; here Serbs and Montenegrins had constituted only 15–20 per cent of the recruit intake, with 30 per cent Kosovar-Albanians, 20 per cent Croats, 10 per cent Bosnian-Moslems and 8 per cent Slovenes. Meanwhile, increasing numbers of non-Serb and non-Montenegrin officers were resigning their commissions, and conscripts were refusing to report for training.

From March 1991, Gen Adzic dismissed or compulsorily retired all non-Serb and non-Montenegrin generals and many other officers in order to ensure loyalty. Most of the Slovenes and Croats enlisted in the Slovene TO or Croatian National Guard (ZNG). By the end of 1991 the JNA was almost exclusively Serbian and Montenegrin; but many were nonetheless reluctant to fight to retain Slovenia and those parts of Croatia outside the traditional Serbian settlement areas. As hostilities commenced in Slovenia on 27 June 1991 many of the multi-ethnic units were rendered ineffective when key Slovene personnel refused to fight. Meanwhile, the JNA was reluctant to deploy too many Serbian troops outside Serbia, when they might be needed to fight nationalist insurrections in Vojvodina or Kosovo. With communism in retreat across Eastern Europe many JNA personnel also objected to serving in a communist army, prompting the government to abolish communist-inspired flags and the red star on JNA cap badges on 16 Oct 1991. However, these gestures did not solve the crises of manpower and morale, or a shortage of weapons – partly caused by seizures from JNA armouries by Slovene and Croatian forces. The JNA could have defended multi-ethnic Yugoslavia from a conventional NATO or (more likely) Warsaw Pact invasion; but it proved unable to fight what was effectively a civil war.

The Yugoslav Air Force did not use its superiority to full advantage against either Slovenia or Croatia, undertaking only limited air-strikes. This *Pukovnik* wears the M55 blue service uniform, with M55 gilt officers' cap badge, M65 collar patches with a gilt eagle, and M82 shoulder straps. Note the pilot's qualification badge on the right breast pocket. (Emil Smutni)

11

Reorganization, 1992

On 30 Dec 1991 the JNA was reorganized following the evacuation of Slovenia at the end of October, and in anticipation of the ceasefire with Croatia signed on 2 Jan 1992. At this time 5 Military District and Naval District were dissolved and the troops transferred to Serbia, Montenegro, Bosnia-Herzegovina and Macedonia. Four military districts were established, supervising 16 numbered and named corps and corps-status 'operational groups'. Of the 17 corps existing in June 1991, 11 had been retained under their old names, four redesignated, one new corps (Mechanized) raised, and two (Ljubljana, Varazdin) disbanded:

1 Military District (Belgrade) N Serbia, Vojvodina, and NE Bosnia-Herzegovina. *Corps:* Mechanized, Kragujevac, Novi Sad, Sabac (ex-Maribor), Tuzla, Uzice

2 Military District (Sarajevo) Rest of Bosnia-Herzegovina. *Corps:* Banja Luka, Bihac (ex-Zagreb), Sarajevo; ex-Ljubljana and Rijeka troops; Knin Operational Group (ex-Knin); ex-N Theatre HQ troops

3 Military District (Skopje) S Serbia, Kosovo and Macedonia. *Corps:* Bitola, Kumanovo, Nis and Pristina

4 Military District (Titograd) Montenegro and SE Bosnia-Herzegovina. *Corps:* Titograd and Trebinje-Bileca Operational Group (ex-Rijeka).

The Naval District HQ was moved from Split to Kumbor in Montenegro, supervising the former 9 Naval Sector. The three Air and AA corps were retained, with 5 Corps moving from Zagreb to Bihac.

On 18 Sept 1991 Macedonia declared its independence, and by 27 March 1992, 30,000 JNA troops had peacefully evacuated the new republic. On 7 Apr 1992 Bosnia-Herzegovina also declared independence. Recognizing that the old six-republic Yugoslavia was dead, the remaining two republics (Serbia and Montenegro) were reconstituted on 27 Apr 1992 as the post-communist Federal Republic of Yugoslavia (SRJ). On 8 May 1992 the JNA was redesignated the Army of Yugoslavia (*Vojska Jugoslavije* – VJ), and the same day began to evacuate about 14,000 troops from Bosnia-Herzegovina, leaving about 80,000 troops to form the Bosnian-Serb Army (VRS). The 165,600-strong JNA had halved, to form the 80,000-strong VJ.

SLOVENE FORCES, 1991

In spring 1991 Slovenia had a population of c.1,966,000. Although only the fifth most populous of the six Yugoslav republics it was the most industrialized, with the highest per capita income in Eastern Europe; Slovenes regarded themselves as central Europeans, close to Austria and Croatia and far removed from Serbia. The population was listed as 1,730,068 ethnic Slovenes (88 per cent), 157,278 Croats (8 per cent), 47,184 widely dispersed Serbs (2.4 per cent), and 31,456 Hungarians and Italians (1.6 per cent). Slovenes are Roman Catholics; their language is distinct from Serbian or Croatian, and uses the Latin alphabet.

Slovenia's armed forces comprised the **Territorial Defence Force** (*Teritorialna obramba* – TO), subordinated in 1988 to 5 Military District in Zagreb. On 8 Apr 1990 Milan Kucan was elected President, with

Janez Jansa as Secretary of Defence. When the TO commander, MajGen Ivan Hocevar (a Slovene), attempted to obey JNA orders to place TO weaponry under JNA control on 15 May 1990, Kucan replaced him with Maj Janez Slapar, officer commanding Upper Carniola District. Local TO commanders concealed some weapons to prevent their confiscation, and in Aug 1990 the Manoeuvre Structure of People's Protection (MSNZ) was established, with police and TO combining to defend the new state.

Major Slapar appointed a new HQ staff, and began transforming the TO from a 70–75,000-strong partially-armed static defence force into an army of 15,000 regulars and 6,000 reservists capable of confronting the JNA. In March 1991 Slovenes of military age were ordered to report for military service, and on 15 May 1990 conscripts commenced basic training at 510 Training Centre at Ig near Ljubljana, and 710 Centre at Pekre. On 2 June they swore allegiance to the Republic of Slovenia.

On 27 Apr 1991 Slapar modified the 1968 TO organization, establishing a General Headquarters (RSTO) in Ljubljana controlling seven Military Districts (PSTO 2–8): 2 (Lower Carniola) District covered the south-east, 3 (Upper Carniola) the north-west, 4 (South Coast) the south-west, 5 (Ljubljana) Ljubljana District, 6 (North Coast) the west, 7 (Eastern Styria) the north-east, and 8 (Western Styria) west-central Slovenia. Each District was divided into 2–5 Military Sub-Districts (hereafter in this text, MSD), totalling 27, each covering up to three local government districts.

By Apr 1991 the Slovenian TO comprised on paper 12 mobile brigades, of which eight (21, 22, 25, 31, 32, 34, 42 & 72) have been identified, and ten independent detachments. The now-Col Slapar planned 11 brigades, with four attached to GHQ and the remaining seven allocated to military districts. However, when hostilities ceased on 7 July 1991 only two of the GHQ brigades – 1 Ministry of Defence Special Bde (*1. Specialna brigada MORiS*) and 9 AA Bde – had been established. 1 Special Bde, formed 17 Nov 1990 from 30 Rapid Deployment Group (*30. razvojna skupina*) under Col Anton Krkovic, was the élite unit, eventually numbering 912 men in three company-sized detachments (I–III) and a reconnaissance unit.

The order of battle in Table 2 is based on the best available data. On 26 June 1991 the Slovene TO comprised 15,707 men, and by 7 July GHQ had partially mobilized reservists, which roughly doubled that number. A brigade was divided into battalions, a battalion (*bataljon*) into companies, a company (*ceta*) into platoons, a platoon (*vod*) into sections, a section (*oddelek*) having about ten men. A group (*skupina*) was a section-sized independent unit. Numbered brigade and battalion sub-units fought independently under Military Sub-Districts, reporting to the Military Districts. Thus there were 60 battalion-sized or company-sized infantry, assault and special duties detachments; 142 infantry and special purpose companies; 240 infantry, special duties, reconnaissance, mortar,

A recruit to the Slovene TO swearing the oath of allegiance to the new Slovene Republic, May 1991; he wears the Slovene MPC-1 helmet with M91 cap badge. (Nigel Thomas Collection)

Table 2: Battle Order of Slovene Territorial Defence Force, 25 June 1991

General HQ (Ljubljana)

Col Janez Slapar
30 Deployment Group/1 Min of Defence Special Bde; 9 AA Bde; helicopter unit; 510 & 710 Trng Ctrs; 130 Tech Institute; Guard of Honour Co

2 Dolenjska (Lower Carniola) Military District (HQ Novo Mesto)

Col Albin Gutman
21 Military Sub-District (Novo Mesto & Trebnje districts), 23 MSD (Crnomelj & Metlika), 25 MSD (Brezice, Krsko & Sevnica), 27 MSD (Ribnica & Kocevje). *Included* 25 Bde, 3x detachments, 8x companies, 7x platoons, 7x groups, MP platoon

3 Gorenjska (Upper Carniola) MD (Kranj)

Col Peter Zupan
31 MSD (Kranj & Trzic), 33 MSD (Radovljica & Jesenice), 35 MSD (Skofja Loka). *Included* 21, 22, 31, 32 & 34 Bdes, 4x dets, 3x cos, 4x ptns, 1 group, MP ptn

4 Juznoprimorska (South Coast) MD (Postojna)

LtCol Vojko Stembergar
41 MSD (Cerknica & Postojna), 43 MSD (Izola, Kopar & Piran), 45 MSD (Sezana), 47 MSD (Ilirska Bistrica). *Included* 5x dets, 3x cos, 11x ptns, MP ptn

5 Ljubljana MD (Ljubljana)

LtCol Janez Lesjak
51 MSD (Ljubljana City), 53 MSD (Logatec & Vrhnika), 55 MSD (Domzale & Kamnik), 57 MSD (Grosuplje & Litija). *Included* 4x dets, 5x cos, 1 AA bty, 8x ptns, 2 groups

6 Severnoprimorska (North Coast) MD (Nova Gorica)

Col Bogdan Beltram
61 MSD (Nova Gorica & Ajdovscina), 63 MSD (Tolmin & Idrija). *Included* 1 det, 1 co, 4x ptns, 6 MD Tank Co

7 Vzhodnostajerska (East Styria) MD (Maribor)

Col Vladimir Milosevic
71 MSD (Maribor, Pesnica & Ruse), 73 MSD (Ljutomer, Gornja Radgona & Ormoz), 75 MSD (Murska Sobota & Lendava), 77 MSD (Ptuj & Lenart), 79 MSD (Slovenska Bistrica). *Included* 72 Bde, 3x bn-strength dets, 26x co-strength dets, 8x cos, 27 AA Bty, 55x pts, 7 MD Tank Co, MP ptn

8 Zahodnostajerska (West Styria) MD (Celje)

LtCol Viktor Kranjc
81 MSD (Celje & Zalec), 83 MSD (Slovenj Gradec, Dravograd, Radlje ob Dravi & Ravne), 85 MSD (Slovenske Konjice, Sentjur & Smarje pri Jelsah), 87 MSD (Trbovlje, Hrastnik, Lasko & Zagorje), 89 MSD (Velenje & Mozirje). *Included* 8x dets, 8 cos, 32 AA Bty, 6x ptns, MP ptn

---

commando, counter-terrorist, intervention, anti-paratroop and rear services platoons; 59 infantry and technical sections; 92 AT groups and 85 blocking groups. Each District HQ included medical personnel and a military police platoon; there were also three AA batteries, and two tank companies formed with captured tanks. The **Air Unit** was formed on 28 June 1991 with 14 UTVA-75 trainers, five Bell 412 and one captured Gazelle SA-341H helicopters, and attached to GHQ. There were no naval units.

Police forces (People's Militia) were controlled by the republics reporting to the Federal Interior Ministry; following the Constitution of 21 Feb 1974 they were entirely independent of Belgrade, and the Slovene Police *(Milica)* reported to the Slovene Interior Minister. On 1 June 1991 there were about 10,000 male and female patrolmen, detectives and paramilitary Special Police *(Posebne enote milice* – PEM) in 13 police districts (Celje, Koper, Kranj, Krsko, Ljubljana city, Ljubljana district, Maribor, Murska Sobota, Nova Gorica, Novo mesto, Postojna, Slovenj Gradec & Trbovlje); plus the Police Protection Unit *(Zascitna enota milice* – ZEM) guarding dignitaries and buildings, and the counter-terrorist Special Police Unit *(Specialna enota milice* – SEM). These reported to the Republican Interior Minister, Igor Bavcar. Slovene Police fought alongside the TO, defending police stations and border crossings.

The **People's Defence Force** *(Narodna zascita* – NZ), wearing civilian clothes with armbands bearing a red star on a blue circle, guarded important factories, buildings and roads; while the uniformed **Civil Defence Force** *(Civilna zascita)* carried out humanitarian duties among the population. The **Slovene Guard** *(Slovenska garda)* was formed from members of the SAMO political party at Maribor in March 1991, but was disbanded by the police that July. Zmago Jelincic's Slovene National

Party (SNS) formed the **Guardsmen** *(Gardisti)* in Ljubljana, but on 30 June 1991 police arrested Jelincic and disbanded the unit.

On 24 June 1991 the Slovene TO mobilized 20,115 troops and police. On 26 June Slovenia declared independence from Yugoslavia, and on 27 June JNA units attacked – convinced, as was the international community, that the infant Slovene Republic would be crushed within a matter of days.

The Ten-Day War

On 27 June 1991, Col Slapar deployed the Slovene TO as follows:

2 District (Lower Carniola, SE Slovenia) covered the central Croatian border, JNA 14 Corps' Crnomelj and Ribnica garrisons, and 31 Corps' Novo Mesto garrison. (Heavy fighting against JNA 4 Armd, 140 Mech and 580 Mixed Arty Brigades.)

3 District (Upper Carniola, N Central Slovenia) covered the western Austrian border, and JNA 14 Corps garrisons at Kranj, Jesenice and Skofija Loka. (Moderate fighting against 1 Armd Brigade.)

4 District (South Coast, SW Slovenia) covered the western Croatian and southern Italian borders, the short Slovene coast, and JNA 14 Corps' Postojna garrison. (Very moderate fighting against 13 Prol Mot Brigade.)

5 District (Ljubljana, Central Slovenia) covered the Ljubljana region, including JNA 14 Corps garrisons at Ljubljana and Vrhnika. (Moderate fighting against 1 Armd Brigade.)

6 District (North Coast, NW Slovenia) covered the northern Italian border, and JNA 4 Corps' Tolmin garrison. (Very moderate fighting against 13 Prol Mot Brigade.)

15

This Slovene TO officer, June 1991, wears the JNA olive-grey M77 field uniform, JNA field officers' shoulder straps without rank stars, and the Slovene mountain cap with the M91 officers' badge. (Nigel Thomas Collection)

7 District (E Styria, E Slovenia) covered the eastern Austrian, Hungarian and eastern Croatian borders, and JNA 31 Corps garrisons at Maribor, Murska Sobota, Ptuj and Slovenska Bistrica. (Heavy fighting against 32 Mech and 195 Mot Brigades.)

8 District (W Styria, E Central Slovenia) covered the central Austrian border, and JNA 31 Corps garrisons at Celje and Dravograd. (Moderate fighting against 195 Mot Brigade.)

Slapar's strategy was to prevent the JNA isolating Slovenia by securing Ljubljana airport and the 35 border crossings with Austria, Hungary, Croatia and Italy. He would also surround the JNA garrisons, occupy the 14 Corps (Ljubljana) and 31 Corps (Maribor) armouries, and block JNA movements within Slovenia by erecting roadblocks. Attempts by 10, 14 & 31 Corps to enter Slovenia from Croatia would be blocked at the border. Croatian President Tudjman did not honour his promise to attack JNA reinforcements entering Slovenia from Croatia, thereby absolving Slovene President Kucan of the obligation to support the Croats during the later Croatian Homeland War.

Although the five corps of JNA's 5 Army had 14 armoured, mechanized or motorized brigades available, only six of these were actually committed (1 & 4 Armd, 32 & 140 Mech, 13 Proletarian & 195 Mot), supplemented by the less suitable 580 Mixed Arty Bde, and elements of the crack 63 Parachute Bde fighting as infantry. Strong JNA garrisons were thereby maintained in Croatia in case Croatian forces supported the Slovenes.

In May 1991 the Serbian LtGen Zivota Avramovic had been appointed commander of the JNA's 5 Army; but Gen Adzic, chief of the

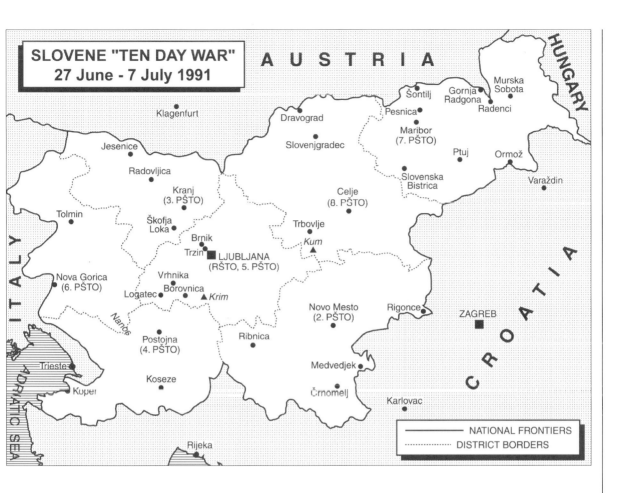

SLOVENE "TEN DAY WAR"
27 June - 7 July 1991

general staff, insisted on conducting the war from 300 miles away in Belgrade, over Avramovic's head – initially Adzic regarded it as essentially a police operation. His strategy was for five JNA brigades to seize Ljubljana's Brnik Airport, Koper seaport and the border crossings, occupy Ljubljana and arrest Kucan's government. His conviction that the insurrection could be crushed easily by conventional tactics led to the error of committing armoured and mechanized sub-units along metalled highways without sufficient infantry support, using unreliable troops reluctant to risk their lives to prevent the secession of a republic not vital to Serbian interests. Thus the JNA exposed itself to ambushes by small groups of determined fighters with an intimate knowledge of the terrain – a classic Yugoslavian scenario. In fact, Adzic never fully unleashed the JNA's destructive firepower, particularly its artillery, leading to a suspicion that President Milosevic was already resigned to Slovene secession. The course of the brief war was as follows:

Thursday 27 June, Day One 5 District troops and police barricaded the 59 roads surrounding Ljubljana. The JNA sent 12 armoured vehicles from 580 Mixed Arty Bde from Karlovac towards Ljubljana, but the column was ambushed at Poganci, on the Slovene-Croatian border, by a counter-terrorist company of 21 MSD, and later near Medvedjek by 21, 23 & 25 MSD units. Meanwhile JNA 140 Mech Bde (Zagreb) was stopped by 25 MSD's Brezice Intervention Group on the Croatian border near Rigonce; ten T-55 tanks from JNA 32 Mech Bde in Varazdin were halted at Ormoz on the Croatian border by 73 MSD, and 41 MSD engaged tanks of 13 Prol Mot Bde at Koseze. JNA 1 Armd Bn from 1 Armd Bde left Vrhnika garrison for Ljubljana's Brnik Airport in two columns of T-55s; the first was engaged by Slovene 1 Special Bde, losing a tank, and was later attacked at Brnik by 31 & 35 MSDs. The second column, reinforced by a helicopter-borne Special Federal Police detachment, was attacked and captured at Trzin by 55 MSD. Meanwhile 51 MSD blockaded the 14 Corps garrison in Ljubljana. Twelve T-55s from 195 Mot Bde headed towards the Austro-Slovene border crossing at Sentilj, but were attacked at Pesnica by 711 Det (71 MSD). 228 Special Duty Co (25 MSD) assaulted JNA 82 Air Bde at Cerklje airfield near Maribor, defended by the JNA 63 Para Bde; but most of the aircraft successfully took off to escape the fighting.

Taking cover from urban firing, this Slovene constable in June 1991 wears the Police work uniform: a 'lead-blue' mountain cap with M91 Police badge, lead-blue trousers, and a grey summer shirt with rank chevrons on the shoulder straps (see rank insignia chart on page 61). He also wears a lead-blue body armour vest, and carries an M70 assault rifle. (Nigel Thomas Collection)

Friday 28 June, Day Two During the night Slovene TO and Police reinforced roadblocks, and attacked border crossings held by the JNA. The JNA 580 Mixed Arty Bde remained under attack at Medvedjek by 21 & 25 MSDs; 73 MSD halted some tanks from 32 Mech Bde at Gibina, and attacked others at the Austro-Slovene border crossing at Gornja Radgona, burning JNA support vehicles. A column from 13 Prol Mot Bde was attacked at Crnice by 61 MSD. JNA 14 Corps was under pressure as the battle for Brnik intensified, with 3 MSD deploying four units (23 Kranjska Gora Co, 1 & 2 Skofja Loka Cos and Radovljica Assault Det) against the JNA 1 Armd Battalion. Borovnica armoury was captured by 27 MSD and 1 Special Bde units; 6 MSD and Slovene PEM units took Rozna Dolina border crossing with Italy, capturing three and destroying two JNA tanks; but 27 MSD and 1 Special Bde units failed to take the Ribnica garrison defended by JNA 14 Mixed Arty Regiment. Meanwhile JNA 195 Mot Bde broke through the Pesnica barricade, but was attacked at Strihovec by 711 Det, other 71 MSD units and Police. Four units of 8 District (2 & 31 Cos; 62 Det, 98 Assault Det) stopped five tanks and 13 other vehicles from 195 Mot Bde near Dravograd, finally capturing the Austro-Slovene border crossing at Holmec. Several Slovene units including 97 Assault Det and 41 & 42 Cdo Ptns attacked the Bukovje garrison near Dravograd. Aircraft of JNA 5 Air Corps attacked TO positions at Brnik, TV transmitters at Krim, Kum and Nanos, the Austro-Slovene border crossing at the Karavanke Tunnel, and 75 MSD's blockade of the 31 Corps ammunition depot at Murska Sobota. Dismayed by the predicament of its isolated columns and garrisons, the JNA declared a unilateral ceasefire.

Saturday 29 June, Day Three Yugoslav Federal Police, with 14 Corps' 289 MP Bn and elements of 63 Para Bde, surrounded at Brnik Airport, surrendered to Slovene 3 District troops. Slovene Police attacked and defeated the JNA 14 Engineer Regt at Skofija Loka in 35 MSD. The JNA 195 Mot Bde column trying to break through to Sentilj surrendered to 7 District units, which formed the captured tanks into the first Slovene armoured unit – 7 District Tank Company. Other JNA units were still surrounded by Slovene TO and Police. A three-man European Community delegation tried unsuccessfully to broker a ceasefire, but in the evening the Slovene parliament voted to accept any peaceful solution with the Federal Government that preserved Slovene independence.

Sunday 30 June, Day Four JNA 10, 13 & 32 Corps regrouped in their Zagreb, Rijeka and Varazdin garrisons before organizing new attacks. Meanwhile, 45 MSD captured 13 Corps' communications centre near Senozece; and 6 District Tank Co was formed from armour captured at Rozna Dolina. 3 District attacked and defeated JNA forces at the Karavanke Tunnel border crossing. That evening the JNA issued a new ultimatum, which was rejected by the Slovene government.

Monday 1 July, Day Five No significant fighting.

Tuesday 2 July, Day Six – the first of the two most decisive days of the war. 21 & 25 MSDs, besieging JNA 580 Mixed Arty Bde at Medvedjek and the Krakovski Forest, finally destroyed this demoralized unit. Meanwhile an armoured battalion from JNA 4 Armd Bde, sent from Croatia to rescue 580 Bde, was itself attacked and captured at Prilipe by 110 Assault Det, despite JNA air support. 73 MSD continued to attack 32 Mech Bde tanks at Gornja Radgona; and 45 MSD captured the Fernetici and Gorjanci Croat-Slovene border crossings from 13 Prol Mot Brigade. Two tank columns of 1 Armd Bde from Vrhnika garrison – one heading towards Ljubljana, the other towards Logatec – were halted at Sinja Gorica and Cesarski Vrh respectively by 5 MSD units. JNA depots at Leskovac, Rajhenav, Prule (Ljubljana) and Zgornja Loznica were captured after heavy fighting. At 2100hrs the Slovene government declared a unilateral ceasefire. General Adzic responded by announcing a final offensive, but resistance to the war was growing in Serbia.

Wednesday 3 July, Day Seven The supposedly élite JNA Proletarian Guards Mech Div left Belgrade to travel the 265 miles along the Belgrade–Zagreb motorway towards Slovenia; but after numerous breakdowns the tank columns ignominiously abandoned the advance. Meanwhile, 73 MSD continued to maul JNA 32 Mech Bde at Radenci and Kog, while 711 Det (71 MSD) and Police defeated 195 Mot Bde at Sentilj without a fight. There were no other engagements; and Gen Adzic agreed to a ceasefire.

Thursday 4 July, Day Eight The Slovene TO now held all border crossings. Under the ceasefire agreement, JNA 5 Army units returned to their Slovenian or Croatian garrisons.

Three days later, on Sunday 7 July, representatives of the Slovene and Yugoslav governments and the European Union met on Veli Brijun island. Under the Brijuni Declaration of 7 July, Slovenia's independence would be finalized on 8 Oct 1991; and on 26 Oct the last JNA troops left Slovenia.

Although called the 'Ten Day War', this conflict actually saw three days of heavy fighting (27–29 June), a two-day lull, two more days of fighting (2–3 July), and three days of ceasefire. There had been 72 armed incidents; the

A Slovene Police *Nizji inspektor* (left) refusing to concede authority to a Yugoslav Federal Police *Samostalni inspector* (right) at Skofije border crossing, June 1991. The Slovene is wearing a grey Slovene Police work uniform and mountain cap; the Federal policeman has the service uniform with light blue summer shirt, lead-blue trousers, and a JNA M59/85 helmet painted Police-blue. See also Plate B3. (Nigel Thomas Collection)

Porocnik **Basic of the Slovene Army in 2003. He wears a leaf-pattern camouflage field uniform with M91 cap badge, subdued name and national breast tabs, and M03 subdued breast rank insignia (see chart on page 58). (Krunoslav Mikulan)**

Slovenes had suffered 19 dead and 182 wounded, the JNA 44 dead and 146 wounded; and 12 foreigners, mostly crews of commandeered lorries, had been killed in a JNA air raid. These absolutely minimal casualties for a war of national independence were testimony to the poor morale of JNA units.

* * *

Slovenia rapidly organized itself as a fully functioning democracy and competitive liberal economy conforming with Western standards; on 29 March 2004 it became the first ex-Yugoslav state to join NATO, and on 1 May the European Union.

On 14 Jan 1995 the TO was redesignated the Slovene Army (*Slovenska vojska* – SV), although the existing organization was retained. In 2005 the SV comprised about 9,000 male and female volunteers in ten ground force brigades – 1, 1 Special, 9 AA, 22, 32 Mountain, 42, 52, 62, 72 & 82. SV units participated in NATO/EU operations in Afghanistan, Bosnia-Herzegovina and Kosovo. The Air Unit was redesignated 15 Air Bde on 9 June 1992, with four squadrons at Cerklje and Brnik. The Slovene Navy (*Ratna mornarica*), based at Koper with about 500 personnel, was formed on 30 Jan 1993, as a coastal defence detachment, renamed in 1997 as 430 Naval Battalion. The Slovene Police (*Slovenska policija*) number about 4,500.

CROATIAN FORCES, 1991

In spring 1991 Croatia had a population of c.4,784, 300, as the second largest republic after Serbia. These included 3,736,356 ethnic Croats (78.09 per cent), 581,663 Croatian-Serbs (12.15 per cent) and 466,246 others (9.74 per cent). Croatia, too, considered itself to be a central European state with historic links to Austria; Croatians are Roman Catholics, while Croatian-Serbs are Serbian Orthodox. The Croatian language has similar grammar and vocabulary to Serbian, but uses the Latin alphabet. Croatia in 1991 comprised the capital Zagreb and 102 districts, reorganized on 29 Dec 1992 into Zagreb and 20 counties, subdivided into 419 districts.

The Croatian Army, 1990–92

On 30 May 1990 President Tudjman controlled the Croatian TO, largely disarmed by the JNA, and the Croatian Police (*Milicija*). On 1 Sept 1990 he appointed Martin Spegelj, former JNA 5 Army commander, as Minister of Defence. Spegelj immediately began covertly buying weapons in East Germany and elsewhere, including 10,000 ex-Hungarian Workers' Guard AK-47 assault rifles from the Hungarian government. On 12 Apr 1991, 1,000 MUP special police and about 9,000 male and female volunteers were organized into the **National Guard Corps** (*Zbor narodne garde* – ZNG). On 15 May, 1 Bde was formed, and on 28 May, 1–4 'A' (Active) Bdes paraded in Zagreb; on the 30th the Guard of Honour Bn in picturesque red uniforms discharged ceremonial duties in Zagreb.

More ZNG numbered brigades, battalions and companies were formed from volunteers. On 15 June 1991 Spegelj took over military command; formation of 'R' (Reserve) brigades was authorized, to suppress the Croatian-Serb insurrection supported by JNA garrisons.

In the period June–Aug 1991 the JNA deployed increasing numbers of troops in Croatia, gradually developing into a full-scale invasion. The ZNG, with four ZNG (formerly A) brigades and 15 R brigades, reorganized as a conventional army; and on 20 Sept 1991 its active units formed the new **Croatian Army** (*Hrvatska vojska* – HV), which on 8 Oct absorbed all R units. The HV was organized into six Operational Zones (1–6), supported by a substantial navy and embryonic air force. The commander, styled chief-of-staff, was Gen Anton Tus (formerly the Yugoslav Air Force commander), with Spegelj 'promoted' to the non-executive position of Inspector-General following disagreements with Tudjman. Appeals to Croatians in the JNA to desert to the HV brought a large influx of trained personnel.

Each Operational Zone (*Operativna Zona*) controlled 0–2 ZNG brigades, 5–16 R brigades, 0–11 independent battalions, and Zone HQ units comprising 1–2 artillery battalions, 1–2 AA battalions, one engineer and one MP battalion. 3 Zone, defending Zagreb, had twice the normal strength; while 1 & 6 Zones, facing the main JNA attack in E Slavonia and Dalmatia respectively, were also heavily equipped.

By 31 Dec 1991 the HV comprised 230,000 men and women – about 180,000 ethnic Croats and 50,000 of other nationalities, including 3,000 non-Serb ex-JNA officers – and 60 brigades were organized. The 1 ZNG 'Tigrovi' (Tigers), 2 ZNG 'Grom' (Thunder), 3 ZNG 'Kune' (Martens) and 4 ZNG Bdes were manned by professional soldiers as a mobile strike force; these were supported by 56 numbered (and sometimes named) brigades of reservists, conscripts and volunteers. Eleven brigades were formed in June 1991 (100, 101, 105–110, 112–114); one in July (111); two in August (103 & 104), and one in September (99). Full mobilization saw 23 formed in October (115, 117–119, 123, 125–134, 137, 138, 145, 148–150, 153 & 204); 15 in November (102, 116, 120–122, 124, 135, 136, 139–141, 143–144, 151 & 154); and two in December (142 & 156). There were also 19 independent infantry battalions (51–57, 61, 65, 74, 76–83 & Dubrovnik); 8 artillery battalions (1, 3, 11, 15, 19, 21, 23

Detail from a photo of Croatian TO, ZNG and NZ personnel parading in summer 1991, wearing Croatian Police leaf-pattern camouflage uniforms. The locally-made badge on the left sleeve is a 'crested Spanish' chequered shield set on a Yugoslav blue-white-red national tricolour flag – this was worn by all three organizations in 1991. (Krunoslav Mikulan)

Croatian badges. (Top, left to right:) Police M90b cap badge – post-1945 Croatian red-and-white chequered shield of 'baroque' style, on gold rays – note that the chequers of the post-1945 shield had a red top-left square ; Police/ZNG M91 baroque shield with gilt crest, and silver or gilt rays, in gold wreath; ZNG & HV M91 baroque shield with gilt crest and *troplet* wreath. (Bottom, left to right:) TO M91 cap badge, worn in north-west Croatia – straight-sided 'Spanish' chequered shield, with coloured crest featuring the shields of Croatia's five historic provinces of Croatia proper, Dubrovnik, Dalmatia, Istria and Slavonia; HV M93 'Spanish' shield with crest and gilt edging; HV 9th 'Wolves' Bde cap badge – gilt sword under silver wolf's head, on a chequered shield with narrow gilt, medium silver, and broad gilt *troplet* edging, the unit's name engraved on a silver scroll. (Krunoslav Mikulan)

& 24); 11 AA units (50 & 101 Rgts; 1, 55 & 61–66 Bns; 58 Co); 7 engineer battalions (33, 34 & 36–40); and 7 MP battalions (66–72). The élite 'Zrinski' Special Forces Bn was attached to the Ministry of Defence. On 17 Oct 1991 Judicial Police personnel (*Pravosudna policija* – PP) formed a company under 1 OZ, which on 20 Jan 1992 became 98 Brigade.

A brigade was supposed to muster 1,800 personnel but under battlefield conditions might have anything between 500 and 2,500. A ZNG motorized brigade had HQ troops (engineer and MP companies; reconnaissance, signals, commando and counter-terrorist platoons),

Table 3: Battle Order of Croatian Army, 31 Dec 1991

GHQ (Zagreb)

1 Operational Zone (Osijek)

3 ZNG Bde 'Martens'; 106, 130, 135 & 160 Bdes (Osijek); 108 & 157 Bdes (Slavonski Brod); 107 Bde (Valpovo); 109 Bde 'Storks' (Vinkovci); 122 Bde (Djakovo); 123 Bde (Pozega); 124 Bde (Vukovar, based Zagreb); 131 Bde (Zupanja); 132 Bde 'Pride of Slavonia' (Nasice); 136 Bde (Podravska Slatina); 139 Bde (Slavonski Samac).
S&S: 3 Arty Bn, 62 AA Bn & 68 MP Bn (Osijek); 19 Arty Bn (Virovitica); 63 AA Bn & 37 Eng Bn (Slavonski Brod); 64 AA Bn (Djakovo); 65 AA Bn (Vinkovci)

2 OZ (Bjelovar)

104 Bde (Varazdin); 105 Bde & 55 Bn (Bjelovar); 117 Bde & 61 Bn (Koprivnica); 127 Bde (Virovitica); 52 & 79 Bns (Daruvar); 54 Bn 'Zrinski' (Cakovec); 76 Bn (Pakrac); 77 Bn (Grubisno polje).
S&S: 15 Arty Bn (Krizevci); 19 Arty Bn

(Virovitica); 24 Arty Bn (Daruvar); 1 AA Bn (Bjelovar); 61 AA Bn (Koprivnica); 58 AA Co (Djurdjevac); 34 Eng Bn (Cakovec); 69 MP Bn (Bjelovar-Koprivnica)

3 OZ (Zagreb) 66 MP Bn (Min of Defence)

1 ZNG Bde 'Tigers', 99–102 Bdes, 83 Bn (Zagreb); 2 ZNG Bde 'Thunder' & 53 Bn (Dugo Selo); 103 Bde (Zabok); 120 Bde 'Ban Tomo Bakac', 57 & 80 Bns (Sisak); 121 Bde (Nova Gradiska); 125 Bde (Novska); 140 Bde (Jastrebarsko); 144 Bde (Zagreb-Sesvete); 145 Bde 'Oaks' (Zagreb-Dubrava); 148 Bde (Zagreb-Trnje); 149 Bde (Zagreb-Tresnjevka); 150 Bde (Zagreb-Crnomerec); 151 Bde (Samobor); 153 Bde (Velika Gorica); 51 Bn (Vrbovec); 56 Bn (Kutina); 65 Bn (Ivanic-grad); 74 Bn (near Petrinja); 78 Bn (near Glina); 81 Bn; 82 Bn.
S&S: 1 Arty Bn, 55 AA Bn, 36 Eng Bn (Sisak); 11 & 21 Arty Bns, 50 AA Rgt, 33 & 38 Eng Bns, 67 MP Bn (Zagreb); 23 Arty Bn (Sunja)

4 OZ (Karlovac)

110 & 129 Bdes, 70 MP Bn (Karlovac); 137 Bde (Duga Resa); 143 Bde (Ogulin)

5 OZ (Rijeka)

111 & 128 Bdes (Rijeka); 118 Bde (Gospic); 119 Bde (Pula); 133 Bde (Otocac); 138 Bde 'Mountain Lynxes' (Delnice); 154 Bde (Pazin).
S&S: 101 AA Rgt & 71 MP Bn (Rijeka)

6 OZ (Split)

4 ZNG Bde, 114 Bde 'Scorpions' & 141 Bde (Split); 112 Bde (Zadar); 113 Bde (Sibenik); 115 Bde (Imotski); 116 Bde 'Neretva Pirates' (Metkovic); 126 Bde (Sinj); 134 Bde (Biograd na moru); 142 Bde (Drnis); 156 Bde (Makarska); Independent Bn (Dubrovnik).
S&S: 66 AA Bn, 40 Eng Bn, 72 MP Bn (Split); 39 Eng Bn (Dubrovnik)

Croatian soldiers parade in Cakovec in summer 1991. Most are NZ personnel, wearing old JNA camouflage caps, jackets and trousers with a yellowish tinge. The M91 shield-&-tricolour sleeve badge is repeated in locally-made cut-down form on the left breast as a straight-sided 'Spanish' shield with 'HRVATSKA' (Croatia) lettered on a top strip. The private at left wears a Croatian Police tiger-stripe camouflage field uniform; on his left breast pocket is a badge of the Croatian chequered shield in a circular *troplet* wreath – note this worn on the sleeve of the man in the right background. (Krunoslav Mikulan)

1st–4th Bns (infantry), and mixed artillery, armoured mechanized and AA battalions. An infantry battalion (*bataljun*, later *bojna*) had HQ troops (signals and security sections, engineer, support, artillery and supply platoons), and 1st–4th Cos; each company (*ceta*, later *satnija*) had

Table 4: Battle Order of Croatian Army, May–Aug 1995

GHQ (Zagreb)

1 Guards Corps (directly subordinate to President):
1 Combined Gds Bde, 1 Gd of Honour Bn, 2 Gds Garrison Bn, 3 Naval Gd of Honour Bn, 4 Gds Special Duties Bn; General Staff Special Forces

Osijek Corps Region

3 Gds Mot Bde 'Martens', 106 & 130 Bdes, 5 & 9 Home Defence Rgts & 261 Recce Co (Osijek); 5 Gds Mot Bde 'Falcons', 11 & 109 HDRs (Vinkovci); 81 Gds Bn 'Godfathers' (Virovitica); 122 Bde (Djakovo); 123 Mot Bde (Pozega); 10 HDR (Vukovar-Vinkovci); 107 HDR (Valpovo), 108 & 157 HDRs (Slavonski Brod); 121 HDR (Nova Gradiska); 125 HDR (Novska); 131 HDR (Zupanja); 132 HDR (Nasice); 136 HDR (Podravska Slatina).
S&S: 2 Arty Bn (Djakovo); 4 Arty Bn, 201 AA Bde, 251 Sig Co & 68 MP Bn (Osijek); 19 Arty Bn (Virovitica); 3 AT Bn (Slavonski Brod); 32 Eng Bn (Nasice)

Bjelovar Corps Region

104 Bde & 24 HDR (Varazdin); 105 Bde & 265 Recce Co (Bjelovar); 52 HDR (Daruvar).

S&S: 16 Arty Bde, 255 Sig Co & 69 MP Bn (Bjelovar); 15 AT Bde (Krizevci); 34 Eng Bn (Cakovec)

Zagreb Corps Region

66 MP Bn (Zagreb – Min of Defence).
1 Gds Mot Bde 'Tigers'; 99–102, 144, 145, 148–150 Bdes; 1 HDR & 262 Recce Co (Zagreb); 2 Gds Mot Bde 'Thunder' & 57 Bde 'Marijan Celjak' (Sisak); 103 Bde, 21 HDR (Zabok); 151 Bde (Samobor); 153 Bde (Velika Gorica); 12 HDR (near Petrinja); 17 HDR (Sunja); 20 HDR (Velika Buna, Glina); 125 HDR (Novska); 140 HDR (Jastrebarsko).
S&S: 6 Arty Bn (Sisak); 8 Arty Bn, 5 AT Bn, 202 AA Bde, 33 Eng Bde & 67 MP Bn (Zagreb); 40 Sig Rgt (Samobor – General Staff); 252 Sig Co (Velika Buna)

Karlovac Corps Region

13 HDR & 266 Recce Co (Karlovac); 14 HDR (near Slunj); 137 HDR (Duga Resa); 143 HDR (Ogulin).
S&S: 10 Arty Bn, 256 Sig Co & 70 MP Co (Karlovac)

Gospic Corps Region

9 Gds Mot Bde 'Wolves', 118 HDR & 263 Recce Co (Gospic); 111 Mot Bde 'Dragons', 128 Bde & 8 HDR (Rijeka); 119 Bde (Pula); 133 HDR (Otocac); 138 HDR (Delnice); 154 HDR (Pazin); 155 HDR (Crikvenica).
S&S: 12 Arty Bn, 203 AA Bde & 71 MP Bn (Rijeka); 253 Sig Co (Gospic)

Split Corps Region

4 Gds Mot Bde 'Lions', 114 Bde 'Scorpions', 6 HDR & 264 Recce Co (Split); 112 Bde, 7 HDR (Zadar); 113 Mot Bde, 15 HDR (Sibenik); 115 Bde (Imotski); 118 HDR (Metkovic); 126 HDR (Sinj); 134 HDR (Biograd na Moru); 142 HDR (Drnis); 156 HDR (Makarska); 163 HDR (Dubrovnik).
S&S: 14 Arty Bn (Primosten); 16 Arty Bn (Dubrovnik); 11 AT Bn (Zadar); 204 AA Bde, 254 Sig Co & 72 MP Bn (Split)

(**Key:** HDR = Home Defence Regiment)

80 men in 1st–4th Ptns and a supply platoon; each platoon (*vod*), 3–4 sections, and each section (*desetina*) about 12 men. A mixed artillery battalion (*divizion*, later *divizijun*) had one 105mm howitzer and two 120mm field gun batteries, while AA battalions had two batteries, each battery (*baterija*, later *bitnica*) of two platoons. An armoured mechanized battalion had one mechanized and two tank companies, each with two platoons. A motorized brigade usually had four infantry and one artillery battalions and as many other troops as available; however, 109 'Storks' Bde (Vinkovci) had six battalions, and 2 Bn had seven companies.

The Croatian Army, 1992–95

Twelve brigades were formed after the Yugoslav-Croatian ceasefire on 3 Jan 1992: two in 1 OZ – 157 (Slavonski Brod) & 160 (Osijek); five in 3 OZ – 98 & 161, later 57 (Sisak), 162 (Petrinja), 165 (Sunja) & 175 (Zagreb); one in 5 OZ – 155 (Crikvenica); and four in 6 OZ – 158 & 164 (Split), 159 (Zadar) & 163 (Dubrovnik).

General Anton Tus was dismissed as chief-of-staff on 22 Nov 1992 after a policy disagreement with President Tudjman, and replaced by Gen Janko Bobetko, who retired on 15 July 1995 and was succeeded by Gen Zvonimir Cervenko. Meanwhile Spegelj retired as Inspector-General on 1 Jan 1993. Tudjman, the Commander-in-Chief (*Vrhovnik*), reduced the size of the Croatian Army following the ceasefire in Jan 1992, demobilizing 20,000 personnel in March, 100,000 in May and June and 40,000 by 15 November. With the help of ex-US Army officers the HV was reorganized into a more streamlined force of 105,000 with 100,000 reservists. The ZNG brigades and independent battalions were

Croatian ZNG reservists take the oath of allegiance in Zagreb, 28 May 1991. They wear JNA M77 uniform; the Croatian mountain caps display M91 Police/ZNG badges, and on the left side a gilt oak-leaf sprig – a badge that was only ever worn on this one occasion. They wear the ZNG badge on the left upper sleeve with the inscription folded from view; and carry a Romanian version of the 7.62mm AKM assault rifle, with a distinctive forward pistol grip. (Nigel Thomas Collection)

A tank crew from the armoured battalion of 7th 'Pumas' Guards Motorized Bde, at Varazdin. They wear the brigade's distinctive orange-brown beret with a gilt puma-head badge; the green-grey tank overalls display the brigade badge on the right upper sleeve and the HV badge on the left. Note the breast rank insignia – see chart on page 59. (Krunoslav Mikulan)

renamed 'Guards', as manoeuvre units with career personnel; and conscripts in 'territorial' brigades gradually converted into 'Home Defence' *(Domobranstvo)* regiments, a regiment *(Domobranska pukovnija –* hereafter in this text, HDR) having three battalions.

The six Operational Zones now controlled 0–2 Guards Mot Bdes, 2–15 Mot Bdes and Home Defence Regts, 0–3 independent Guards battalions, and corps HQ units – 0–3 artillery battalions, 0–2 AT brigades or battalions, 0–1 AA brigades, 0–1 engineer brigades or battalions, a signals and a reconnaissance company and an MP battalion. Zagreb Corps District remained the largest, with extra units. In Feb 1993 the Operational Zones were redesignated Corps Districts; and the élite 1 Guards Corps, reporting directly to President Tudjman, was formed on 1 Apr 1994.

In May 1995 the Guards Corps comprised 1 Mixed Guards Bde (three battalions plus artillery, armour, and Mi-24 combat and Mi-8 transport helicopters) plus special bodyguard units. The original four ZNG brigades were redesignated Guards Motorized Brigades in Dec 1992, and three more were added: 5 'Sokolovi' (Falcons), formed 25 Oct 1992; 6, later 9 'Vukovi' (Wolves), 1 Nov 1992; and 7 'Pume' (Pumas), 23 Dec 1992. The 19 independent infantry battalions were disbanded, and five independent Guards battalions (80–84) were formed.

There were 43 Home Defence regiments (HDR) and 34 brigades: 15 new regiments (1, 4–5, 7–8, 11, 13–17, 20, 21, 24 & 52); five regiments formed from brigades with new numbers (129 > 3, 141 > 6, 135 > 9, 124

ABOVE LEFT **ZNG** personnel parading in May 1991. They wear dark blue Yugoslav Navy berets, jackets and trousers, with Russian-style blue-and-white striped undershirts; the cap badge is the M91 Police/ZNG type. Again, they carry Romanian AKM rifles. The rank-and-file have light brown leather belts, the officer (right foreground) a dark brown belt and cross strap. (Nigel Thomas Collection)

ABOVE RIGHT **ZNG** personnel parade to take the oath of allegiance in May 1991. These men and women wear grey Police work uniforms, with the M91 Police/ZNG cap badge and curved M90 'POLICIJA' sleeve title. (Nigel Thomas Collection)

A Croatian MP NCO on duty. Note black beret with MP falcon badge, repeated on a fob buttoned over the left breast pocket of his leaf-pattern camouflage suit; white-on-black 'MP' brassard; tombstone-shaped left sleeve badge; and the breast rank insignia. An instructor's badge is pinned to his right pocket flap. (Krunoslav Mikulan)

> 10, 162 > 12); 23 regiments formed from brigades and retaining the brigade number (107–110, 116, 118, 121, 125, 126, 132–134, 136–138, 140, 142, 143, 154–157 & 163); and 30 existing brigades (99–106, 112, 114–115, 119, 122, 128, 130, 131, 144, 145, 148–151, 153, 158–160, 164–165, 175 & 204). Four brigades were disbanded (98, 117, 120 & 127); three became motorized brigades (111, 113 & 123), one an independent motorized battalion (139), and 161 Bde was redesignated 57 Brigade. The eight artillery battalions expanded to ten (2, 4, 6, 8, 10–12, 14, 16 & 19). There were two AT battalions (3 & 5) and two brigades (15 & 16); four AA brigades (201–204); two engineer battalions (32 & 34) and one brigade (33); one signals regiment (40) and six companies (251–256).

The Military Police was initially organized into seven battalions (66–72), with five companies serving with 'A' Brigades, one attached to Navy GHQ, three platoons with Air Force GHQ and about 60 platoons with 'R' brigades. 8 MP Light Assault Bde was formed in Sept 1993, but in Apr 1994 its personnel transferred to 1 Mixed Guards Brigade. In Jan 1993 five MP counter-terrorist units were created – a company within 66 Bn and platoons in 67, 68, 71 and 72 Battalions. In 1995 the Military Police comprised six battalions (66–68, 71–73) and three companies (69, 70 & 74); 73 Bn was attached to the Navy, 74 Co to the Air Force.

Other Croatian military forces

Almost all the Yugoslav seaboard came within Croatian territory. The **Croatian Navy** (*Hrvatska ratna mornarica* – HRM) was formed 12 Sept 1991 with about 1,000 men from the Yugoslav Navy (JRM), under command of Adml Sveto Letica. By May 1995 it had expanded to about 1,850 personnel, comprising 1 Bde with two missile ships, a torpedo-boat and a minelayer, and logistics, submarine and commando ship detachments; and two River Forces brigades. The Marine Infantry was reorganized into infantry companies, 53 Cdo Co, Home Defence battalions and coastal artillery batteries, 96 Missile Base, 51 Signals Bn and 73 MP Battalion.

The **Croatian Air Force** (*Hrvatsko ratno zrakoplovstvo i protuzracna obrana* – HRZ i PZO) was officially formed in Jan 1992, but Col Tomo Madic

ABOVE LEFT **A Croatian Police** *Samostalni inspektor* transferred to the ZNG, summer 1991. He wears a US Army summer camouflage uniform and the M91 ZNG/HV cap badge. His rank insignia are a combination of the M86 and M91 Police systems – the bars and piping conform to the 1986 regulations, and the six-point star to the 1991 regulations. (Nigel Thomas Collection)

ABOVE RIGHT **The Croatian Interior Minister, Ivan Vekic,** in 1991, wearing a camouflage uniform with the MUP M91 shield badge on the left upper sleeve, and the new shoulder strap rank insignia, introduced in July 1991 but not generally issued until January 1992. It resembled the M86 pattern, with dark blue shoulder straps piped in gold for Interior Ministry officials (blue piping for lower ranks), and gold six-point stars above 10mm & 20mm gold bars. The M91 rank badges were worn until 1996. (Nigel Thomas Collection)

ABOVE LEFT **Josip Lucic, one of the first commanders of the Croatian Special Police, in 1991.** With his US Army winter-weight camouflage uniform he wears a Croatian tiger-stripe field cap displaying the M90b Police cap badge. He later became the commander of the ZNG 1st 'Tigers' Brigade; at the time of writing he holds the position of the Chief of the Armed Forces General Staff. (Nigel Thomas Collection)

ABOVE RIGHT **Members of the Croatian Special Police in early 1991.** On their US Army surplus uniforms note the M90b cap badge and the M90 curved 'POLICIJA' sleeve title. The right-hand man has a Soviet 7.62mm Dragunov sniper rifle. (Nigel Thomas Collection)

(later BrigGen Imra Agotic) had assembled a nucleus of 150 pilots, air and ground crews and AA artillerymen in time for the war in 1991. These had formed three air squadrons and three independent air platoons, flying captured JNA and commandeered civilian aircraft. By May 1995 there were four airbases with eight squadrons, missile AA and air

RIGHT **Alija Siljak, a HOS commander at Vukovar in November 1991, and leader of the HOS 'Black Legion'.** He wears standard Croatian US Army camouflage, with the controversial black circular HOS sleeve badge described in the commentary to Plate E3. (Emil Smutni)

surveillance brigades, and signal and MP companies.

On 8 Nov 1990 Tudjman took over nominal command of the **Croatian Territorial Defence Force** (*Territorijalna obrana* – TO) from the JNA. Most of the 240,000 Croatian TO personnel outside the Croatian-Serb autonomous regions transferred to the ZNG or HV individually or in 1,200-strong TO brigades, while some TO units continued to operate under Croatian command. On 5 Apr 1991 the **People's Defence Force** (*Narodna zastita* – NZ) was formed, eventually comprising over 100,000 civilian volunteers organized into detachments, companies and platoons subordinated to HV brigades or local district 'crisis HQs'. Their mission was to guard state property and utilities, strategic installations and convoys, and report enemy movements. The NZ was disbanded in March–April 1992, many personnel transferring to *Domobranstvo* (Home Defence) units.

Croatian Police

On 30 May 1990 there were 16,000 Croatian Police (*Milicija*, from 8 Nov 1990 *Policija*) subordinated to the Republican Secretariat (from 8 Nov 1990, Ministry) of Internal Affairs (*Ministarstvo unutarnjih poslova* – MUP), in 17 Secretariats covering Zagreb and 102 local government districts. Almost 60 per cent of the Croatian police force had been Croatian-Serbs, and after the Serb rebellion in Aug 1990 many of these deserted to the Krajina Police, forcing Tudjman to appeal to Croats to join. On 5 Aug 1990 about 1,800 police candidates (predominantly Croat) started training in Zagreb, and on 12 Sept the best were transferred to the new Special Purpose Unit (*Jedinica za posebne namjene*), in Dec 1990 renamed the Lucko Counter-Terrorist Unit (*Anti-teroristicka jedinica* – ATJ – Lucko). The other trainees formed named battalion-strong Special Purpose Units: 'Lucko', 'Rakitje', 'Tuskanac', 'Kumrovec' and 'Dubrava', and later 'Tomislavov dom' and 'Vinica'.

By Jan 1991 the MUP was hugely expanded, with 55,260 personnel: 21,360 regular police, 22,900 police reservists, plus 11,000 Special Police. In May 1991 'Rakitje', 'Kumrovec', 'Tuskanac' and 'Dubrava' formed the Special Police Bde; but two weeks later most Special Purpose Units were reorganized into 'A' brigades of the National Guard Corps (ZNG), with 'Rakitje' forming the cadre for 1 ZNG Brigade. In June 1991 the Police were reorganized into 19 Police Departments (PUs). By late July 1991 there were about 40,000 regular police and reservists plus 4,000 Special Police, taking much of the strain of the early fighting in summer 1991 and continuing to figure significantly in Croatia's defence capability. In 1992 the Special Purpose Units were redesignated Special Police Units (*Specijalne jedinice policije* – SJP), with one attached to each of 17 out of 19 police departments. On 26 Dec 1992 the Police were reorganized into 20 county police departments, 18 of them with an SJP.

In July 1990 the **Croatian Civil Defence Force** (*Civilna zastita* – CZ), formed to assist in civil emergencies and commanded by Josip Slunjski, was reorganized as part of the MUP, with about 90,000 personnel organized into companies, platoons and sections.

A young Croatian Special Policeman photographed following the first armed clash between Croatian and Serbian-Krajina forces in the Lika region, March 1991. With a US Army winter camouflage uniform he wears body armour and a Slovene MPC-1 helmet. (Nigel Thomas Collection)

HOS personnel in 1991. The militiaman in the foreground wears a HOS black field beret with pre-1945 coat of arms badge, and a non-standard camouflage jacket in brown, light grey, dark grey and green. Note that the HOS sleeve badge is worn on the left breast by the man on the left. The use in HOS insignia of the pre-1945 chequered shield, with the white top-left square, was criticised for the association with the Ustasha militia of World War II. (Emil Smutni)

Croatian paramilitary forces

In Feb 1990 Dobroslav Paraga reformed the Croatian Party of Rights (HSP) as an extreme nationalist party acting as an apologist for the Ustasha régime of World War II. In 1991 a paramilitary wing was formed, the **Croatian Defence Forces** (*Hrvatske obrambene snage* – HOS), under Ante Paradzik, later MajGen Blaz Kraljevic. 'HOS' deliberately recalled the initials of the combined Ustasha-Croatian Army of 1944–45, and the HOS wore insignia evoking the NDH period. The militia claimed 10,000 men (the Croatian government estimated 2,000), organized in understrength 'battalions' and including the 300-strong Black Legion (*Crna legija*) at Vukovar under Alija Siljak. The HOS gained a reputation for fanatical bravery in combat at Dubrovnik and Vukovar, and for ruthless mistreatment of Croatian-Serb civilians. Tudjman arrested Paraga in Nov 1991; the HOS was disbanded on 21 Dec, some personnel integrating with the HV, including its 109 & 114 Brigades.

The HOS was the only organized Croatian paramilitary force, although temporary self-defence units were formed locally, and absorbed into local ZNG or Police units when these were sufficiently organized. Before the war some political parties, particularly the HDZ, planned covert groups to resist a JNA invasion, but these never took the field.

About 100 **foreign volunteers** – American, British, Canadian, Croatian emigré, French, German, Hungarian, Italian and Scandinavian – fought in the ZNG, HV and HOS, usually for adventure or the Croatian cause, and some defended Osijek in Nov 1991. A Spanish journalist, Edouardo Flores, formed '1 International Platoon' at Ernestinovo (E Slavonia) in Nov 1991, disbanded in spring 1992.

SERBIAN KRAJINA FORCES

The Krajina or Knin-Krajina Region, the largest and most compact Serb minority community in Croatia, covered ten districts: four in northern Dalmatia (Benkovac, Drnis, Knin, Obrovac), three in Lika (Donji Lapac, Gracac, Korenica), and three in Kordun (Slunj, Vojnic, Vrginmost), with Knin as the capital. These were joined in Aug 1990 by the four districts of the Banija, later Banovina (Dvor na Uni, Glina, Kostajnica, Petrinja). In July 1989, encouraged by Serbian President Milosevic, Krajina Serbs had formed the 'Initial Committee of Serbs of Northern Dalmatia, Lika, Kordun, Banija, Slavonia and Baranja', followed on 6 May 1990 by the 'Serbian Forces HQs of Kordun, Banovina [Banija renamed] and Lika'. On 21 Dec 1990, Milan Babic, leader of the Serbian Democratic Party (SDS), proclaimed the Serbian Autonomous Region of Krajina (SAO), and on 21 Feb 1991 this entity formally seceded from Croatia.

On 16 Aug 1991, Serbs in parts of three districts in W Slavonia (Nova Gradiska, Novska and Pakrac) proclaimed the 'SAO Western Slavonia' (capital Okucani); and on 25 Aug 1991 two districts in E Slavonia (Beli Manastir, Vukovar) proclaimed the 'SAO Slavonia, Baranja and Western Syrmia' (capital Erdut, later Vukovar). On 19 Dec 1991 all three regions were united as the Republic of Serbian Krajina (RSK), with Knin as capital, and Goran Hadzic (from 25 Jan 1994, Milan Martic) as President. The RSK area was 6,575 square miles (30 per cent of Croatia's area), with a population of 555,550 (12 per cent of Croatia's), including 331,619 Croatian-Serbs (60 per cent of the RSK population but only 57

Two contented recruits of the Krajina Army in 1992, wearing brown TO M70 berets with M92 Krajina Police badges, comprising a red-blue-white Serbian tricolour on a gilt ornamental backing. (Croatian Ministry of Defence)

per cent of the total number of Croatian-Serbs) and 168,026 Croats (30 per cent). The RSK was a territorially fragmented, economically unviable pseudo-state, dependent on an increasingly disengaged President Milosevic, and increasingly vulnerable to the Croatian Army.

At the time of the Croatian-Yugoslav ceasefire of 3 Jan 1992, Croatian forces had retaken the Pakrac district of W Slavonia, but this, and the rest of the RSK, was henceforth supervised by the United Nations. In May 1995 the HV retook the rest of W Slavonia, and Knin-Krajina in August. The RSK was formally abolished on 7 Aug 1995, although E Slavonia continued as the 'Region of Syrmia and Baranja' under UN control until 15 Jan 1998, when it was peacefully reintegrated into the sovereign republic of Croatia.

Blurred but interesting photograph of Krajina Army personnel parading in 1993 in JNA camouflage uniforms, wearing a beret with the M92 eagle badge (see page 42), and a curved sleeve title with Cyrillic lettering 'JURISNA BRIGADA' ('Assault Brigade'). Note the three gold braid chevrons on the left breast patch of the sergeant in the foreground. (Croatian Ministry of Defence)

The Krajina Serb Army

The Croatian-Serb TO units in Knin-Krajina, W Slavonia and E Slavonia had retained their light weapons after 14 May 1990; later about 12,000 men from the TO brigades, supplemented by paramilitary units and volunteers (including some Greeks and Russians), formed the Krajina Territorial Defence Force (*Teritorijalna odbrana SAO Krajine*).

On 16 Oct 1992 the Krajina TO was redesignated the Serbian Army of the RSK (*Srpska vojska Republike Srpske Krajine* – SVRSK) and later the Serbian Krajina Army (*Srpska vojska Krajine* – SVK), under LtGen Milo Novakovic, with 35–40,000 personnel. The army was divided into four Krajina Corps (7, 15, 21 & 39); one W Slavonian (18), and one E Slavonian (11). These six corps controlled 26 brigades: one armoured (2); two motorized (75 & 92); two light infantry (18 & 103); 20 infantry (9, 11, 13, 19, 24, 26, 31, 32, 40, 45, 51, 54, 70, Knin, Korenica, Obrovac, Vrlika, plus three others); and one mixed artillery. Each corps HQ had an MP company.

(Continued on page 41)

Table 5: Battle Order of Serbian Krajina Army, May–Aug 1995

GHQ (Knin)

Special Forces Corps:
71 Special Bde, 2 Guards Bde, 2 Armd Bde, Special Police Bde

7 (North Dalmatian) Krajina Corps (Knin)

1 Lt Bde (Vrlika), 2 Inf Bde (Djevrske), 3 Inf Bde (Benkovac), 4 Lt Bde (Obrovac), 75 Mot Bde (Knin), 92 Mot Bde (Zemunik); MP Co (Knin)

11 (East Slavonian) Krajina Corps (Vukovar)

Baranja Div (Beli Manastir): 37 Inf Bde (Bilje), 39 Inf Bde (Beli Manastir). 35 Bde (Dalj), 40 Inf Bde (Borovo), 43 Inf Bde (Tenja), 45 Inf Bde (Ilok)

15 (Lika) Krajina Corps (Korenica)

9 Mot Bde (near Medak), 18 Inf Bde (Bunic), 50 Inf Bde (Vrhovine), 70 Inf Bde (Plaski), 103 Lt Bde (Donji Lapac); MP Co

18 (West Slavonian) Krajina Corps (Okucani)

51 Inf Bde (Pakrac), 54 Inf Bde (Okucani), 98 Inf Bde (Rajic); 59 Detachment, 63 Detachment; MP Co (Okucani)

21 (Kordun) Krajina Corps (Vojnic)

11 Inf Bde (Vojnic); 13 Inf Bde (Slunj), 19 Inf Bde (Vrginmost); 212 Border Detachment; Armd Bn; MP Co (Vojnic)

39 (Banija) Krajina Corps (Petrinja)

24 Inf Bde (Glina), 26 Inf Bde (Kostajnica), 31 Inf Bde (Petrinja), 33 Inf Bde (Dvor); MP Co (Petrinja)

YUGOSLAV NATIONAL ARMY, 1991–92
1: *Razvodnik*, 269th Mountain Bde; Slovenia, June 1991
2: *Vodnik I. klase*, 12th Proletarian Mech Bde; Eastern Slavonia, October 1991
3: *Kapetan I. klase*, 29th Armd Bde; Banija, Croatia, November 1991

3

2

1

SLOVENE FORCES, JUNE–JULY 1991
1: *Major*, 31 MSD, Territorial Defence Force, Brnik Airport
2: *Desetnik*, Brezice Co, 25 MSD, TO, Medvedjek
3: *Inspektor*, Slovene Police, Sentilj

B

SERBIAN MILITIAS
1: *Dobrovoljac*, Chetnik Detachments; Croatia, 1991
2: *Pukovnik*, Serbian Volunteer Guard; Vukovar, November 1991
3: *Dobrovoljac*, Serbian Guard; Gospic, September 1991

CROATIAN FORCES, 1991
1: *Vojnik*, 'Marko Kovac' Detachment, Territorial Defence Force; Cakovec, September 1991
2: *Policajac specijalac*, 'Rakitje' Special Purpose Unit; Plitvice, March 1991
3: *Policajac I. klase*, Dubrovnik Police Department; November 1991

3

2

1

D

CROATIAN FORCES, 1991
1: Officer, 106th Bde, National Guard Corps; Osijek, September 1991
2: *Vojnik*, 129th Bde, Croatian Army; Karlovac, December 1991
3: Officer, HOS Militia; Vukovar, October 1991

E

SERBIAN KRAJINA FORCES, 1991–95
1: *Vodnik*, Krajina Territorial Defence Force, 1991
2: *Brigadni djeneral*, Serbian Krajina Army, 1993
3: *Stariji milicionar*, Krajina Police Field Force, 1994

CROATIAN FORCES, 1991–95
1: *Pripadnik*, People's Defence Force, October 1991
2: *General-pukovnik*, Croatian Army, 1993
3: *Vodnik*, Military Police Counter-Terrorist Unit, 1994

CROATIAN FORCES, 1995
1: *Narednik*, 121st Home Defence Regt; Nova Gradiska, May 1995
2: *Bojnik*, 7th Guards Bde; Knin, August 1995
3: *Zapovjednik*, Zadar-Knin Special Police Unit, August 1995

2

3

1

H

Krajina Police on parade in 1991, wearing Serbian Police tiger-stripe camouflage berets, shirts and trousers, with JNA conscripts' light brown leather belts and shouldering M70 automatic rifles. (Croatian Ministry of Defence)

Lieutenant-General Milan Celeketic took over command in 1994, but following the loss of W Slavonia on 3 May 1995 he was replaced by the former JNA deputy chief-of-staff, LtGen Mile Mrksic. The SVK had about 40,000 men, still organized in six corps, but including the independent Baranja Division. There were now 27 brigades: three motorized (9, 75 & 92); one light infantry (103); two 'light', presumably also infantry (1 & 4); 19 infantry (2, 3, 11, 13, 18, 19, 24, 26, 31, 33, 37, 39, 40, 43, 45, 50, 51, 54 & 98); and two undesignated, presumably infantry (35 & 70). There were also a border detachment (212 Det) and two undesignated, presumably infantry detachments (59 & 63 Detachments). In June 1995 four élite brigades – 2 Armd, 2 Guards, 71 Special, and Special Police – formed the Special Forces Corps.

After the Croatian Operations 'Flash' and 'Storm' the remaining SVK units in the Region of Syrmia and Baranja were disarmed and disbanded by the UN by 21 June 1996.

Other Krajina forces

A small force of SVK motorboats patrolled the 'Novigrad Sea' – actually a lagoon, east of Zadar. The JNA 105 Air Regt transferred from Zadar to Udbina, where it formed 105 Air Bde of the SVK Air Force and AA Artillery, operating helicopters and MiG-21 jet fighters; to comply with UN ceasefire requirements the helicopters re-formed in Jan 1992 as the Krajina Police Helicopter Squadron.

From July 1990 to Jan 1991 police in Krajina broke away from the Croatian Police and formed the Krajina Police (*Milicija Krajine*), nicknamed 'Martic's Men' (*Marticevci*) after its commander, Milan Martic, the Knin police chief. From 21 Dec 1990 he was Krajina's Minister of Internal Affairs, until his appointment as President in Feb 1994. (Martic was indicted at the UN War Crimes Tribunal at the Hague for ordering the firing of Orkan rockets at Zagreb in May 1995.) The Krajina Police claimed 7,000 regulars and 20,000 reservists in July 1991, and was organized into seven Secretariats (SUPs): Knin, Korenica, Petrinja and Vojnic (Knin-Krajina); Okucani (W Slavonia), and Beli Manastir and Vukovar (E Slavonia).

There were also Special Police (*Specijalne jedinice milicije* – SJM) units, the most famous being the 1,000-strong '*Knindze*', led by the notorious 'Captain Dragan' Vasiljkovic, which raided Croatian-held Zadar district in 1990 and fought at Vukovar in Nov 1991. In Feb 1993 Vasiljkovic established an SJM training centre at Knin, and in June 1995 the SJM formed a brigade in the Special Forces Corps.

From 1 July 1996 the Region of Syrmia and Baranja was under the Transitional Police Force (*Prijelazna policija*) formed from Serbs, Croats and minorities under UN supervision. On 15 Dec 1997 this force formally merged with the Croatian Police.

Detail of the Serbian Krajina Army M92 eagle badge, worn on a dark blue beret. (Croatian Ministry of Defence)

SERBIAN MILITIAS IN CROATIA

In 1991 five Serbian opposition political parties formed six paramilitary militias to support Milosevic's ambitions in Croatia. Except for the Serbian Guard, all these were financed and organized by Serbian State Security (SDB), and fought under JNA tactical command. They were collectively called 'Chetniks' or 'terrorists' by the Croats and Western media, while the Serbs called them 'territorials' or 'volunteers'. By July 1991 these militias had about 12,000 men – ex-JNA officers and NCOs, former communist activists and local Serbian farmers – many of whose leaders hailed from the Serbian criminal underworld.

The militias rarely attacked well-defended Croatian towns (Vukovar was the exception), preferring to conduct mopping-up operations behind JNA units and in non-Serb villages. Sometimes they directed other militias, and occasionally JNA units. They fought at Osijek, Sisak and Karlovac, and in Baranja, E Slavonia and N Dalmatia. Politically motivated irregular forces almost invariably commit atrocities; although 'ethnic cleansing' – altering a region's ethnic composition by terrorizing civilians into fleeing as refugees – was also practised by Croats, Bosnian-Muslims and Kosovar-Albanians, these Serbian militias gained a particular reputation for cruelty (which blinded the international community to the real privations suffered by many innocent Croatian-Serbs at other hands).

The infamous 'Captain Dragan' Vasiljkovic of the Krajina-Serb 'Knindze' SJM battalion, wearing a tiger-stripe camouflage beret and shirt. The beret badge is an improvised Serbian white cross with four contraposed Cyrillic 'S' characters (see commentary to Plate C1). He wears non-standard rank insignia, comprising three JNA rank stars worn Police-style in a triangular arrangement. (Nigel Thomas Collection)

The **Serbian Chetnik Movement** (*Srpski cetnicki pokret* – SCP), named after Gen Mihailovic's resistance army during World War II, was established in late 1990 by Vojislav Seselj, the extreme nationalist head of the Serbian Radical Party (SRS). Although it probably never exceeded 185 members, the SEP earned a bloody reputation in E Slavonia from 1 Apr 1991. They claimed responsibility for the deaths of 12 Croatian Special Police at Borovo Selo on 2 May 1991; attacked Croatian villages in Beli Manastir (Baranja) in Aug 1991 and in Podravska Slatina (W Slavonia) in September, around Vukovar from October, and at Skabrnja near Zadar in November. They also participated in savage fighting in Banovina.

The **White Eagles** *(Beli orlovi)* were formed in late 1990 and led by Dragoslav Bokan of the Serbian People's Renewal Party (SNO), reporting to the Serbian Interior Ministry in Vojvodina. They attacked villages in Slatina (W Slavonia) in Sept 1991, Lovas in October and Vukovar in November. Personnel wore a white eagle on a red shield on the left upper sleeve.

The **'Dusan the Mighty'** *(Dusan Silni)* militia, named after the greatest Serbian medieval king (r.1331–55), were also under Bokan's control. They transferred to E Slavonia in Apr 1991 and were implicated in the Borovo Selo incident in May. They also fought at Lovas in Oct 1991 and Vukovar that November.

The **Serbian Guard** (*Srpska garda* – SG) were formed in June 1991 by Vuk Draskovic's Serbian Renewal Movement (SPO). This 1,500-man militia, with at least three battalions (1–3), was led by Djordje Bozovic-Giska, later by Branislav Lainovic-Duga, and recruited mainly from Serbs in Vojvodina. The SG were ill-equipped and poorly trained, and co-operated reluctantly with the communist-indoctrinated JNA. They fought at Nova Gradiska (W Slavonia), and participated in the attack on Gospic (Lika).

The **Serbian Volunteer Guard** (*Srpska dobrovoljacka garda* – SDG), nicknamed 'Tigers' (Tigrovi), were the armed wing of the neo-communist 'League of Communists – Movement for Yugoslavia' (SK-PJ), led by Slobodan Milosevic's wife Mirjana Markovic. Formed on 11 Oct 1990, and a political rival to the Serbian Guard, it numbered 500–1,000 combatants. Led by the notorious Zeljko Raznjatovic – 'Arkan' – and based at Erdut near Vukovar, the well-armed SDG (it even had some tanks) operated in E Slavonia, and its special units led the assault on Vukovar in Aug 1991. The SDG field commander was killed on 15 Sept near Gospic. In Feb 1993 the SDG fought near Benkovac (N Dalmatia).

The Serbian Democratic Party (SDS) formed a unit under Miso Radulovic at Vukovar in Nov 1991; and also Milan Paroski's Serbian Volunteer Detachment *(Srpski dobrovoljacki odred)*, and Mirko Jovic's Volunteer Detachments *(Dobrovoljni odredi Mirka Jovica)* from Nova Pazova.

THE CROATIAN HOMELAND WAR

Croatian ZNG volunteers from the Baranja-Medjimurje Bn pose for a group photograph in Cakovec in summer 1991. They are wearing Croatian Police pattern uniforms in leaf camouflage, with JNA conscripts' leather belts. The majority of the officers and men of this battalion came from the ranks of refugees 'ethnically cleansed' from north-eastern Baranja by Krajina-Serb forces. (Krunoslav Mikulan)

Croatia's war of independence, known in Croatia as the Homeland War, divided into four phases:

(1.) 17 Aug 1990–2 July 1991:
Increasing Serb/Croat tension in Croatia.
(2.) 3 July 1991–2 Jan 1992: Croatian resistance to the JNA, Serb militias and SVK in E and W Slavonia, Banovina, Lika and Kordun, and Dalmatia.
(3.) 3 Jan 1992–30 Apr 1995: The 'phoney war' of limited Croatian operations against the Republic of Serbian Krajina (RSK).

(4.) 1 May–7 Aug 1995: Croatian
      Operations 'Flash' and 'Storm' in
      W Slavonia and Knin-Krajina.

Defence Minister Spegelj organized six
Operational Zones (OZs) to confront the
JNA and Serbian militias attacking from
Serbia, Bosnia-Herzegovina and Monte-
negro, the JNA garrisons in Croatia, and
Croatian-Serbs in the three Autonomous
Regions (SAOs):

1 OZ (Osijek) covered Eastern Slavonia.
Confronting JNA corps from Serbia and
Bosnia-Herzegovina, and Krajina TO
forces in E and W Slavonia, required 19
Croatian brigades to be raised.

2 OZ (Bjelovar) covered W Slavonia and
northern Croatia proper. With no borders
with JNA-held territory, the only threat
was SAO W Slavonia; only seven brigades
were formed.

3 OZ (Zagreb) covered Zagreb Region
and Banovina, including the northern
part of SAO Krajina. It faced JNA forces
from Bosnia-Herzegovina and Krajina TO
forces in Banovina; 15 brigades and many
HQ units were raised.

4 OZ (Karlovac) covered Kordun Region, partly in SAO Krajina, and
formed 11 brigades to confront JNA and Krajina TO forces.

5 OZ (Rijeka) covered Rijeka Region, Gorski Kotar and parts of Lika
region (Gospic and Otocac), forming eight brigades.

6 OZ (Split) covered the narrow Dalmatian territory, vulnerable to
JNA forces in Montenegro and Bosnia-Herzegovina and to Krajina TO
units in northern Dalmatia; it raised 13 brigades.

All armies are subject to political control, but Croatian generals
frequently complained that President Tudjman intervened on the
battlefield, placing political manoeuvrings above strategic advantage.

Two members of an NZ guard
unit join civilians in reporting for
military duty in summer 1991;
they wear camouflage uniforms
with a yellowish tinge. Note the
Croatian M91 shield-&-tricolour
sleeve badge, and JNA officers'
'Sam Browne'-style belt.
(Krunoslav Mikulan)

Increasing Serb-Croat tension

On 17 Aug 1990 Croatian-Serb villages around Knin, Benkovac and
Obrovac (N Dalmatia), and in September in Banovina, posted armed
guards and blocked traffic in the 'log revolution', asserting the
independence of the Serbian Autonomous Regions and defying
Croatian police. On 15 Feb 1991 the SCP abducted Croats in Osijek
District, and on 1 March 1991 Krajina police briefly occupied Pakrac
police station (W Slavonia). On 31 Mar the Plitvice National Park
(Lika), occupied by Serbian SDS activists, was retaken by Croatian
Police, led by 'Lucko' ATJ and 'Rakitje' Special Unit. In Apr 1991
Serbian militias incited Croatian-Serbs to rebellion, while local JNA
garrisons intervened to support the insurgents under the pretext of
restoring order. The Croatian Police station at Dalj (E Slavonia) was
abandoned under attack by JNA tanks and Serb militias.

In Apr 1991 Croatian HDZ extremists fired a rocket into the Croatian-Serb village of Borovo Selo near Vukovar (E Slavonia); on the night of 30 Apr/1 May 1991 the SCP and Dusan Silni militias wounded two Croatian policemen and abducted two others; and on 2 May they ambushed a bus, killing 12 Croatian Osijek Special Police reinforcements and wounding 33 others. TV footage of their mutilated bodies enraged the Croats and shocked the international community. Meanwhile, JNA tanks from Petrinja garrison (10 Corps) entered Banovina, attacking Dvor na Uni and Kostajnica. On 6 May, Croat civilians in Split attacked a JNA armoured column, killing a soldier; in June, Glina police station (Banovina) was wrecked, and SCP and SDG attacked Kraljevcani, near Petrinja. The Krajina and Slavonian countryside erupted into hundreds of local firefights, as Serbs and Croats battled for local supremacy, with the Croatian Police and ZNG vainly attempting to stem the violence.

The Eastern Slavonian Front

Eastern Slavonia comprised seven districts largely under Croatian control (Djakovo, Nasice, Osijek, Slavonski Brod, Valpovo, Vinkovci and Zupanja), and two (Beli Manastir and Vukovar) in the SAO Slavonia, Baranja and W Syrmia.

This flat, open region, ideal for armoured warfare, came under the Croatian 1 Operational Zone, with BrigGen Karl Gorinsek committing 19 brigades (1 & 3 ZNG, 105–109, 121–124, 130–132, 135, 139, 157, 160 & 204). There were three JNA 17 (Tuzla) Corps garrisons, at Osijek, Djakovo and Vinkovci, and the Croatians also faced Krajina TO brigades and Krajina Police in Beli Manastir and Vukovar districts. The JNA 12 (Novi Sad) Corps, reinforced by 252 Arm Bde from 24 Corps, were across the River Danube in Vojvodina and northern Serbia; and 17 Corps and 14 (Ljubljana) Corps units were beyond the River Sava in Bosnia-Herzegovina. JNA strategy was for 12 & 17 Corps to catch Croatian forces in a pincer movement, meeting 5 (Banja Luka) Corps advancing from W Slavonia. The Croats intended to defend Vukovar and Osijek and control the E Slavonian sections of the Belgrade-Zagreb motorway and Drava Highway.

OPPOSITE **Croatian Military Policeman at Turanj, near Karlovac, in April 1992. He wears a black beret, a leaf-pattern uniform and a white MP's belt. Note the obsolete ZNG MP badge on his left upper sleeve: on a deep arc of black, bordered with white, a centred chequerboard shield has white lettering 'POLICIJA' above, and is flanked by 'ZNG' and 'RH' – for 'ZNG Police, Republic of Croatia'. (Henrik Clausen)**

On 3 July 1991, JNA 12 Corps reached Beli Manastir district (Baranja) and advanced south, followed by the SCP. Meanwhile 252 Armd Bde entered SE Slavonia, attacking Vinkovci en route to Vukovar; and by 31 July there was fighting along the entire Danube frontier with Serbia. Croatian ZNG and MUP units surrounded JNA garrisons in Osijek, Djakovo, Vinkovci and Vukovar, while JNA 12 Corps occupied Beli Manastir district. In September the Croatians shelled Vinkovci, and in November attacked the 15,000-strong Osijek garrison (JNA 106, 130, 135 & 160 Bdes), while Croatian 109 & 124 Bdes harassed their supply lines. Meanwhile Croatian 157 Bde defended Slavonski Brod, and 108, 131 & 139 Bdes the Sava riverbank, against two JNA 17 Corps motorized brigades.

From 24 Aug 1991, Vukovar was held by 700 men of the Croatian 204 Bde, the Zrinski Bn, elements of the 1 ZNG Bde, HOS militia and Croatian Police, plus 1,000 armed Croatian and Serbian civilians, commanded by Col Mile 'Jastreb' (Hawk) Dedakovic. The town was besieged by JNA 12 Corps, 252 Armd Bde, Krajina TO, SDG and later White Eagles militias. On 14 Nov the Croats surrounded JNA forces in the Petrova Gora barracks and beat off a 12 Corps armoured relief column, but Tudjman vetoed Gen Gorinsek's relief attempt with 3 ZNG, 106 & 122 Bdes, 109 Bde's Tank Company and Osijek Special Police on 13 October. Major-General Zivota Panic, JNA 5 Military District commander, divided his forces into the Northern and Southern Groups, but the Croats beat off his assault on 16 October. Panic determined to occupy Vukovar at all costs, sending the élite Proletarian Guards Mech Div and 1 Military District's 152 Mixed Arty and 1 Mixed AT Bdes into the final offensive on 2 November. Vukovar was cut off, but Osijek Air Platoon's three Antonov An-2 crop-duster aircraft carried out

A close-up of the Croatian BK-3 helmet with Croatian leaf-pattern cover, which gives this conscript a distinctly US Army look. (Krunoslav Mikulan)

CROATIAN "HOMELAND WAR"
12 August 1990 - 14 December 1995

improvised night-bombing raids against JNA positions. On 12 Nov, Gorinsek's Croatian task force, reinforced by 101 & 105 Bdes, again failed to reach Vukovar; on 18 Nov 1991 Croatian 204 Bde was destroyed and the garrison fell, losing about 3,700 dead and missing, but having killed about 5,000 enemy and destroyed 600 tanks and artillery pieces.

Vukovar became known as 'Croatia's Stalingrad', and TV footage of its utter devastation – genuinely resembling the aftermath of a World War urban battle – shocked the world. Overcoming its 87-day defence had exhausted the JNA 12 Corps and Guards Mech Div, buying precious time for Croatian forces. They stabilized on the Osijek–Vinkovci line; and Osijek, reinforced with heavy weapons seized from JNA garrisons, withstood JNA shelling until the ceasefire on 3 Jan 1992. Croatian forces had held E Slavonia, but were unable to retake the SAO E Slavonia, Baranja and W Syrmia.

The Western Slavonian Front

Western Slavonia was a roughly rectangular area comprising six districts. Bilogora, in the north, consisted of three hilly and mainly Croatian districts – Donji Miholjac, Orahovica and Slatina. The mixed Croat-Serb central Pozega District was dominated by Mt Papuk; and the south, mainly populated by Croatian-Serbs, contained Mt Psunj in Nova Gradiska district. The SAO W Slavonia was a triangular area formed from western Nova Gradiska, eastern Novska and eastern Pakrac.

RIGHT **Members of the élite Croatian ALFA Zagreb Special Police unit in 1995; they wear green shirts, covered BK-3 helmets and combat vests. The yellow-and-brown SJP right sleeve badge is clearly inspired by that of the US Army SF; on the right breast are a round ALFA patch, above the appropriate police department title, above the 'ALFA' title. They carry SAR-80 automatic rifles. (Hallo 92 Collection)**

SAO W Slavonia was garrisoned by the JNA 28 & 31 Partisan Divs, Krajina TO brigades and Krajina Police, supported by Serbian militias, and 5 (Banja Luka) Corps in Bosnia-Herzegovina. There were three JNA garrisons in 2 OZ at Varazdin, Bjelovar and Virovitica. Ten Croatian brigades were eventually deployed against SAO W Slavonia: two (127 & 136) in the north; six (1 ZNG, 101, 104, 105, 117 & 125) in the west; and two (121 & 123) in the east.

The Krajina TO strategy was to bring more Croatian-Serbs within its borders by expanding westwards across Pakrac District and eastwards over Nova Gradiska, and to support the JNA drive northwards across Bilogora to the Hungarian border, thus cutting E Slavonia off from the rest of Croatia. The Croatian strategy was to contain the expansion, keep the W Slavonian sections of the Belgrade-Zagreb motorway and Drava Highway open, and then counter-attack to eliminate the SAO.

There were initially only four Croatian brigades in W Slavonia (121, 125, 127 & 136), so local police and civilian volunteers sustained most of the early fighting. In the north, three Croatian policemen were killed in Daruvar on 20 July 1991, and on 4 Aug Podravska Slatina police station was attacked. In September Serbian forces, including the SCP and White Eagles, occupied Mt Papuk, and were attacking Daruvar with air support from 82 Air Bde in Banja Luka; Podravska Slatina, held by the Croatian 127 & 136 Bdes, was shelled. On 16 Aug Krajina TO troops – supported from early September by JNA units including 329 Armd Bde (5 Corps),

and Serbian volunteers from Bosnia-Herzegovina – seized Okucani, consolidating their hold in the south. In the west, Croatian Police and armed civilians defended the centre of Pakrac and Lipik against JNA and Krajina TO artillery, tanks and infantry, while the Croatian 125 Bde defended Novska. In the east, the Croatian 121 Bde in Nova Gradiska fought off the Serbian advance.

On 31 Oct 1991 the Croatian Army took the offensive. Their 127 & 136 Bdes, in Operation 'Swath-10', advanced southwards from Bilogora, occupying Mt Papuk and destroying the 28 Partisan Div and a White Eagles unit. On 4 Dec five brigades (1 ZNG, 101, 104, 105 & 117) advanced from the north-west and two (121, 123) from the north-east, to cut SAO W Slavonia off from Bosnia-Herzegovina in Operation 'Hurricane 91'. On 26 Dec 1991, with Croatian forces controlling the northern half of W Slavonia and needing perhaps one more day for total victory, President Tudjman – probably foreseeing a peaceful solution to the Croatian conflict – ordered a halt, thereby sparing the SAO until May 1995.

The Banovina Front

Central Croatia proper was defended by the 3 OZ, covering the Zagreb Region, with 12 districts (Donja Stubica, Ivanic-Grad, Jastrebarsko, Klanjec, Krapina, Kutina, Pregrada, Vrbovec, Zabok, Zagreb, Zelina and Zlatar); and also the Sisak (Banovina) Region with six districts, one of them (Sisak) under Croatian control and four (Dvor na Uni, Glina, Kostajnica and Petrinja) in SAO Krajina. The 3 OZ raised 17 brigades (1 & 2 ZNG, 99–103, 120, 125, 140, 144, 145, 148–151 & 153), sending 101 & 125 to W Slavonia and 140 to Kordun. There were three JNA 10 Corps garrisons at Dugo Selo, Petrinja and Zagreb. The Croats faced Krajina TO brigades and Krajina Police in Banovina, and JNA 5 Corps over the River Una in Bosnia-Herzegovina. The JNA strategy was to occupy Zagreb and advance to the Slovene border, splitting Croatia in two and arresting Tudjman's government; but the strength of 3 OZ's assembled forces indicated the Croats' determination to resist.

JNA and Krajina TO forces targeted Croatian-majority towns on the edge of the sparsely populated and hilly Banovina, while Serbian militias terrorized Croatian villages. On 9 July JNA M-84 tanks attacked and occupied Glina, defended by the 2 ZNG Bde and Sisak Special Police, before heading for Petrinja and, on 15 July, Kostajnica. On 2 Sept JNA 5 Corps attacked Petrinja, capturing the town on 26 Sept after heavy street fighting against 2 ZNG Bde, which retreated to Sisak. Meanwhile the isolated town of Kostajnica, under renewed JNA attack since 8 Sept and defended by Croatian ZNG and Special Police – including the famous 'Zebras' (*Zebre*) – fell on 12 September. However, the dogged defence of Sisak by 2 ZNG Bde and 57 Independent Bn, and of the outlying Komarevo and Sunja villages, halted the JNA and Krajina TO units, which lacked the ammunition, supplies and morale for further attacks. The stabilization of the Banovina Front on the River Kupa saved Zagreb, and ensured that an independent Croatian state would survive.

Since July 1991, Croatian forces had surrounded the JNA 10 Corps garrisons, and in September Petrinja and Dugo Selo fell. This left the 'Marshal Tito' garrison, Pleso airbase and other Zagreb garrisons tying down Croatian units, including the élite 1 ZNG Bde. President Tudjman was prepared to assault the garrisons despite his concern over the likely collateral damage to Croatia's capital; but in Dec 1991 the JNA peacefully evacuated Zagreb for Bosnia-Herzegovina.

The Kordun and Lika Fronts

Kordun was defended by 4 OZ with seven districts: four (Duga Resa, Karlovac, Ogulin and Ozalj) under Croatian control, and three (Slunj, Vojnic and Vrginmost) in SAO Krajina. Nine brigades of 4 OZ were deployed in Kordun (103, 110, 119, 129, 137, 138, 140, 143 & 150). The Croats faced Krajina TO brigades, Krajina Police and JNA 13 Corps in

A member of the Croatian 7th Guards Motorized Bde reconnaissance unit, wearing Croatian leaf pattern camouflage with a black woollen cap and black face paint. Note the recce unit badge worn on the left upper sleeve, where the HV badge is normally worn: it features binoculars and a sword. In 1995 this brigade was engaged against Krajina-Serb forces in northern Dalmatia. (Krunoslav Mikulan)

51

Another member of the 7th Guards Mot Bde recce unit wearing an unusual sniper suit, consisting of imitation leaves in light grey and light brown. (Krunoslav Mikulan)

SAO Krajina, and the 10 Corps garrison in Karlovac. The JNA stategy was to advance to the Adriatic, thereby cutting Dalmatia off from the rest of Croatia.

The Lika Region, defended by 5 OZ, comprised five districts: two (Gospic and Otocac) under Croatian control and three (Donji Labac, Gracac and Korenica) under SAO Krajina. The whole 5 OZ comprised the Rijeka Region, Lika, Istria, the offshore islands and the coastal strip, with 19 districts: Buzet, Cabar, Crikvenica, Delnice, Gospic, Krk, Labin, Mali Losinj, Otocac, Pag, Pazin, Porec, Pula, Rab, Rijeka, Rovinj, Senj, Umag and Vrbovsko. There were three JNA 13 Corps garrisons in Croatian-held territory, at Gospic, Pula and Rijeka.

JNA and Krajina TO units, fully engaged in Banovina, could not spare the resources for a full-scale offensive in Kordun. On 14 Sept the Croatian 110 & 129 Bdes blockaded the JNA garrison in Karlovac, and on 4 Oct halted a Krajina TO relief force at Turanj. The Croats cut to pieces a JNA relief column of tanks from 4 Armd Bde outside Karlovac; reinforced by 103 & 150 Bdes and supported by 128 Bde in nearby Duga Resa, they held their positions until the 3 Jan 1992 ceasefire. Croatian enclaves isolated in Krajina Serb territory held out until 22 Oct 1991, when Dreznik and Grabovac fell.

Five Croatian 5 OZ brigades (111, 118, 128, 133 & 154) fought in Lika. There was one JNA 13 Corps garrison in Croatian-held territory at Gospic, and the Croats faced Krajina TO brigades, Krajina Police and JNA 13 Corps in SAO Krajina. On 30 Aug 1991 the Krajina TO in southern Lika attacked Perusic, and on 2 Sept Gospic, held by the Croatian 118 Brigade. On 5 Sept the élite Zrinski Bn, operating north of Gospic, ambushed a JNA tank column from Banja Luka; on the 15th, 118 Bde defeated an SDG unit, and on 18 Sept occupied the Gospic garrison. Meanwhile, Krajina TO forces were shelling the northern Lika town of Otocac, held by 118 Bde and Croatian Police; it was reinforced on 19 Sept by the newly formed 133 Bde and, following the peaceful evacuation of the JNA Rijeka garrison, by 111 & 128 Brigades. By 12 Dec 1991 these units had formed a successful defensive line in central Lika.

The Dalmatian Front

Dalmatia was defended by the 6 OZ, with 22 districts. In northern Dalmatia there were nine districts: five (Biograd na Moru, Sibenik, Sinj, Split and Zadar) under Croatian control, and four (Benkovac, Drnis, Knin and Obrovac) in SAO Krajina. Eleven Croatian brigades were raised in 6 OZ: two (4 ZNG & 114) were deployed across Dalmatia, and six (112, 113, 126, 134, 141 & 142) in northern Dalmatia. There were three JNA garrisons in Croatian-held territory, at Sibenik, Split and Zadar. The Croats were hard pressed by Krajina TO brigades, Krajina Police, Serbian militias, and JNA 9 Corps – under the notorious BrigGen Ratko Mladic – in SAO Krajina. JNA strategy was to occupy the southern Dalmatian coast, giving a future Greater Serbian state an outlet to the Adriatic Sea.

On 15 July 1991 Krajina TO forces from Benkovac advanced towards Biograd na Moru, and on 26 July, 4 ZNG deployed west of Obrovac. On 11 Sept the Croatian-Serbs and JNA reached the bridge at nearby Maslenica, cutting Dalmatia in two and leaving the Pag island ferry as the only link; they destroyed the bridge on 21 November. The powerful JNA 9 Corps forced back the lightly armed Croats, reaching Skradin near Sibenik in August, and occupying Drnis on 16 Sept before being stopped by Croatian 126 Bde near Sinj. Meanwhile, on 15 Sept the Croatian 113 Bde occupied the Sibenik JNA garrison and naval base. 112 Bde, supported by 4 ZNG Bde and Croatian Police, was too lightly armed to threaten JNA forces installed in part of Zadar town, controlling the road to Benkovac in Krajina and backed up by artillery and airpower. The JNA garrison in Split began to evacuate in October, and the port, under bombardment from JRM ships, was reinforced by the Croatian 114 Bde (including the HOS IX Bn) and 4 ZNG Brigade. The JNA made further advances in Nov 1991, but the line stabilized in December, leaving the Croats in Jan 1992 clinging precariously to Zadar, Sibenik, Split and the Adriatic coastal strip.

Southern Dalmatia had 13 districts: eight mainland (Dubrovnik, Imotski, Makarska, Metkovi, Omis, Ploce, Trogir and Vrgorac), and five islands (Hvar, Korcula, Lastovo, Supetar and Vis), defended by three Croatian brigades (115, 116 & 156). The Croats faced JNA 4 Corps from Bosnia-Herzegovina, 2 Corps from Montenegro and Krajina TO forces, intent on occupation.

The importance of Dubrovnik, a city famous since Roman times and well known to foreign tourists, was more symbolic than strategic. 2 JNA Corps (Titograd, Montenegro) and 24 Mot Bde (Trebinje, Bosnia-Herzegovina), reinforced by 6 & 19 Mtn Bdes and 3

Croatian *General bojnik* Miljenko Kruljac, commanding 6 Varazdin Corps District, wearing the light brownish-grey summer service uniform for officers and NCOs. The peaked cap has a broad black chin strap edged gold, gilt HV badge, and gold general officers' oak leaf peak embroidery. He wears general officers' collar patches and M96 black shoulder slides. The pocket fob badge is that of the Ban Jelacic Staff College. (Krunoslav Mikulan)

Partisan Div, commenced the siege of Dubrovnik on 30 Sept 1991; JRM ships began shelling, and on 3 Oct the JNA cut the Adriatic Highway link to the north. Croatian Police and civilian volunteers, later reinforced by the HV Dubrovnik Bn (later 163 Bde) and HOS IX Bn, defended the historic town, while army units and marine infantry formed a defensive line 25 miles north at Ston (Peljesac peninsula) and four miles south at Kupari. They clung to the hills overlooking the city, relying on international outrage to shame the JNA. However, on 15 Oct the JNA 2 Corps occupied Cavtat and proclaimed an embryonic pro-Serbian 'Dubrovnik Republic' under the presidency of Aleksandar Aco Apolonijo. The JNA resumed shelling on 11 Nov, and on 6 Dec began a final assault, before agreeing to a ceasefire under pressure from international opinion.

Croatia's 'phoney war'

The fifteenth ceasefire, signed on 2 Jan 1992 and effective 3 Jan, brought the final withdrawal of the JNA from Croatia. However, the Republic of Serbian Krajina (RSK) – 30 per cent of Croatian territory – was placed under UN control, and parts of southern Dalmatia remained under JNA occupation. On 15 Jan 1992, Croatia was internationally recognized as an independent state, and admitted to the United Nations on 22 May. President Tudjman used the period from January 1992 to April 1995 to strengthen the Croatian economy and political institutions, and to transform the HV into a formidable fighting machine. Meanwhile he maximized the Croatian position in Bosnia-Herzegovina through political initiatives and military intervention, and authorized a series of limited military operations on Croatian soil.

Narednik Suskovic of the Croatian Military Police models the khaki M92 winter service uniform. His cap has a black peak and gold-edged black chin strap; note the gilt 'H-over-V' collar badges, and gilt metal MP falcon badge on his pocket fob; hidden here is a gold-embroidered falcon on his right upper sleeve. (Krunoslav Mikulan)

Despite the ceasefire, southern Dalmatia south of Ston was still occupied by the JNA 2 Army's Trebinje-Bileca Group (redesignated 4 May 1992 as Bosnian-Serb Herzegovinian Corps), which was shelling Dubrovnik, held by the Croatian 163 Brigade. On 18 May 1992, under Operation 'Tiger', six Croatian brigades (1 & 4 Guards, 114–116 & 141) advanced to Dubrovnik along the Adriatic Highway against Serbian units weakened by losses in Herzegovina, finally lifting the siege on 23 October. Meanwhile the Croatian 113 & 142 Bdes, Zrinski Bn and elements of 4 Guards Bde launched a successful attack on the Miljevac Plateau between Sibenik and Drnis on 21–22 June 1992.

On 22 Jan 1993 Operation 'Horned Viper' was launched with three brigades (4, 6 Guards & 112), 72 MP Bn and Home Defence units, with air support from police helicopters, to push the SVK 7 Krajina Corps and White Eagles away from Zadar and retake the Maslenica Bridge. Later 9 Guards Bde, SJP and other units joined the intense fighting; on 25 Jan the bridge was in Croatian hands, and a still-tenuous link with the rest of

Croatia was re-established amid national rejoicing. On 28 Jan 1993, in a parallel action not approved by the government, 126 Bde and 16 HDR retook the Peruca dam and power plant near Sinj, thereby preventing their destruction by the SVK, which would have flooded a large populated area. Finally, on 9 Sept 1993, in Operation 'Medak Pocket', Croatian forces retook Croatian villages in Lika south of Gospic.

Operations 'Flash' and 'Storm', 1995

By 1995 the Croatian Army were ready to retake Krajina, held by the SVK which, Gen Bobetko believed, was now too weak to mount a defence. Croatian Guards Brigades were deployed as strike forces, supported by other brigades and Home Defence regiments.

Operation 'Flash' in May 1995 was the occupation of W Slavonia by 7,200 troops of the Croatian 2 OZ, against the 8,000-strong SVK 18 Krajina Corps. On 1 May elements of eight Croatian units attacked: 5 Guards Bde, 121 HDR, 81 Guards Bn, 105 Bde, 123 Bde tanks and SJP units advanced from the east; 1 & 3 Guards Bdes, and 125 HDR attacked from the west, while 52 HDR held the Pakrac-Pozega line in the north. RSK President Martic ordered SVK forces in Banovina to fire retaliatory Orkan cluster-bomb rockets at Zagreb, Sisak and Karlovac, causing civilian casualties. 18 Krajina Corps swiftly collapsed, and by 3 May the Croats had occupied W Slavonia as demoralized SVK troops and almost all the 15,000 Serb population fled across the Sava river into Bosnia-Herzegovina.

The 4 & 7 Guards Bdes and 126 HDR entered south-central Bosnia on 25 July 1995, occupying Bosansko Grahovo in Operation 'Summer 95', ready to attack the Krajina capital of Knin from the rear. Operation 'Storm', 4–7 Aug 1995, was launched with 130,000 Croatian troops in the Guards Corps, five Guards brigades, 14 other brigades and 21 Home Defence regiments – a total of 41 major units, against about 30,000 SVK troops. The offensive was preceded by a heavy artillery barrage along the entire front.

Eleven Croatian units attacked SVK 39 Krajina Corps in Banovina. 125 HDR took Dubica, and 17, 121 & 151 HDR captured Kostajnica on the eastern flank, while 2 Guards Bde, 153 Bde and 20 HDR occupied

Petrinja and Glina on the western flank. Meanwhile the main force, comprising 57 Bde and 12, 101 & 103 HDR, advanced across the Zrinska Gora mountains, taking Gvozdansko and Dvor na Uni.

Kordun was a smaller operation, with six Croatian units confronting 21 Krajina Corps. 1 Guards Bde dominated the battlefield, occupying Slunj with 14 & 143 HDR, Vojnic with 110 & 137 HDR and 104 Bde in support, then Vrginmost and Topusko, and linking up with Bosnian-Moslem 5 Corps in the besieged Cazinska Krajina region of Bosnia-Herzegovina.

The largest attack was in Lika, where fifteen Croatian units advanced against 15 Krajina Corps. In the north, 1 Guards Bde took Saborsko supported by 99 Bde and 133, 138 & 143 HDR, while 119 Bde and 154 HDR captured Petrovo Selo. Meanwhile in central Lika, 8, 133 & 138 HDR took Vrhovine, and 128 Bde Korenica. In the south, 9 Guards Bde, and 8, 118, 154 & 157 HDR with SJP units, supported by 111 & 150 Bdes from Gospic, captured Donji Lapac, and the Guards Corps and 4 & 9 Guards Bdes captured Srb.

Eleven Croatian units advanced against 7 Krajina Corps in N Dalmatia: 4 & 7 Guards Bdes attacked from Bosnia, supported by 6 & 142 HDR, and captured Knin; 9 Guards Bde took Obrovac; 112 Bde, Karin; 7 HDR, Benkovac; 134 HDR, Ervenik; 15 & 113 HDR, Mokro Polje, and 144 Bde and 126 HDR, Kijevo.

The Croatian Army regained 4,050 square miles of territory in 'Storm', confirming its military efficiency. It was also a major factor, however, that Serbian President Milosevic had decided to sacrifice the RSK to achieve a Serb-Croatian peace settlement, and forbade the VJ or the Bosnian-Serb Army (VRS) to support the Krajina forces. Meanwhile, about 150–200,000 Krajina Serbs (up to 78 per cent of the 255,000 RSK Serb population) retreated with the SVK into Bosnia. Film of these tractor convoys horrified the world; their flight depopulated and economically crippled Krajina – the 450-year-old Serbian community in Croatia had effectively ceased to exist. Croatian troops were accused of brutality towards Serbian civilians and 'ethnic cleansing', and the operational commander, LtGen Ante Gotovina, was later indicted by the Hague International Tribunal; he was arrested in December 2005.

* * *

The Dayton Agreement of 14 Dec 1995 marked the end of the Croatian Homeland War. Economic devastation, and international suspicions about President Tudjman and the conduct of Croatian troops in the RSK and Bosnia-Herzegovina, made Croatia's path towards a Western European-style democracy and liberal economy longer and more tortuous than it had been for Slovenia. However, Tudjman's death on 10 Dec 1999, the election of the internationally more acceptable President Stjepan Mesic on 27 Jan 2000, and an improving economy, all brought the prospect of eventual NATO and EU membership closer.

The Croatian Army is still organized on the 1992 model, but with the Guards brigades fully mechanized, more specialized units and fewer motorized infantry, and the Guard Corps disbanded. It is supported by the Navy (HRM), the Air Force (HRZ) and the Police. Croatian contingents were serving in Afghanistan at the time of writing.

THE PLATES

A: YUGOSLAV NATIONAL ARMY, 1991–92

A1: *Razvodnik*, 269th Mountain Brigade; Slovenia, June 1991

Mountain troops wore the peaked mountain cap and cloak instead of the sidecap and greatcoat. A new uniform was introduced in the mid 1980s based on the M77 model, comprising a jacket with no shoulder straps, reinforced shoulders and concealed buttons, reinforced trousers, climbing boots, woollen socks and leather anklets. The left breast pocket rank insignia were wider than the standard pattern: officers, 8–10cm; NCOs, 5cm; and troops – like this senior private – 4cm. The M59 helmet, issued in 1961, was slightly modified in 1985 as the M59/85, and worn with a red star until Oct 1991.

A2: *Vodnik I. klase*, 12th Proletarian Mechanized Brigade; Eastern Slavonia, October 1991

The M77 brownish-grey worsted uniform was introduced in 1982, but the coarse cloth M53 uniforms were worn until 1991. The tunic had four flapped pockets and plastic

Rank insignia of Yugoslav People's Army

(Note: Insignia used by **JNA & Yugoslav Army (VJ)** to 3 Feb 2003; and by **Serbian Krajina Army (Krajina TO, SVRSK & SVK)** from June 1990 to 7 Aug 1995).
Insignia were worn on uniform-colour **shoulder straps** of officers' and career NCOs' M55 service tunic, greatcoat & raincoat; conscript NCOs' and privates' tunic & greatcoat; and all ranks' M77 field jacket, and M75 (or older) summer shirt. Metal or braid insignia were worn on uniform-colour patches on the **left breast pocket** of all ranks' mountain jacket, parka & cloak; camouflage field jacket, greatcoat & summer shirt, tank & paratrooper overalls. Buttons, gold for officers & NCOs, green-grey for privates.

General officers (1–4) *Shoulder straps:* 3mm embroidered gold leaf edging, sword-&-baton in wreath, 4–1 generals' stars. *Breast:* gold metal sword-&-baton in wreath, 4–1 bars.

Field officers (5–7) *Shoulder straps:* double 3mm gold braid edging, 3–1 gold metal officers' stars. *Breast:* 3–1 narrow gold metal bars over one broad bar.

Captains & subaltern officers (8–11) *Shoulder straps:* 3mm gold braid edging, 3–1 gold metal stars. *Breast:* 4–1 narrow gold metal bars.

Warrant & non-commissioned officers (12–17) *Shoulder straps:* 2–1x 3mm gold braid chevrons, 4–1 gold metal officers' stars. *Breast:* 4–1 narrow gold metal chevrons over 1–0 broad chevrons.

Privates (18–21) *Shoulder straps:* 3–0x 4mm red braid chevrons. *Breast:* 3–1 red braid chevrons; (21), no insignia.

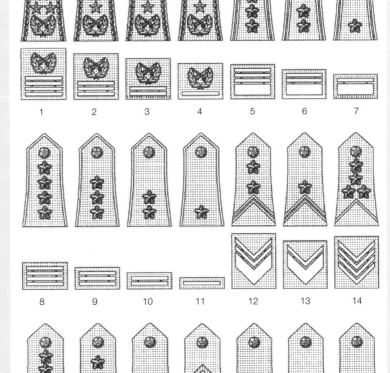

(Drawings by Darko Pavlovic)

Key to ranks:

1. General armijo
2. General-pukovnik (SVK 22.4.1993–94: Armijski djeneral)
3. General-potpukovnik (SVK 22.4.1993–94: Divizijski djeneral)
4. General-major (SVK 22.4.1993–94: Brigadni djeneral)
5. Pukovnik
6. Potpukovnik
7. Major
8. Kapetan I. klase
9. Kapetan
10. Porucnik
11. Potporucnik
12. Zastavnik I. klase
13. Zastavnik
14. Stariji vodnik I. klase
15. Stariji vodnik
16. Vodnik I. klase
17. Vodnik
18. Mladji vodnik (SVK 22.4.1993–94: Narednik)
19. Desetar
20. Razvodnik
21. Vojnik

buttons. The M77 winter coat, replacing the greatcoat, had two side pockets, cuff fastenings, belt, shoulder strap rank insignia and two inside pockets – lower back for the pullover or removable lining, and left front for the detachable hood. The summer uniform in lighter material comprised the M75 shirt (replacing the coarser M53) or a better quality M75 walking-out shirt, trousers, and field cap with M49 badges – red star for privates, with silver pentangular rays for officers and NCOs; members of 'Proletarian' units, like this senior sergeant, added a hammer-and-sickle. Officers and NCOs wore a dark brown superior quality leather belt and crossbelt, privates (conscripts) a lighter brown belt and two shoulder braces.

A3: *Kapetan I. klase*, 29th Armoured Brigade; Banija, Croatia, November 1991
Camouflage uniforms were introduced in the mid 1980s. The pattern illustrated was issued to paratroopers, then special units, reconnaissance troops and finally infantry. The jacket had four retaining chest D-rings, two zippered breast pockets, flapped pockets on the waist and left upper arm, and breast rank insignia on a rectangular camouflage patch. Later variants had no breast pockets, or only one D-ring on the left chest; there was an olive-grey pattern uniform for paratroopers, military police and special units, and a lead-blue

pattern for some Krajina police. Standard JNA badges were worn on the beret, paratroop officers wearing a small red star over a parachute in a wreath. The cap badges introduced in Oct 1991 were, for NCOs and privates, a gold JNA or TO monogram on a horizontally divided blue-white-red disc, on gold crossed swords; officers like this captain wore it on a silver rosette, general officers adding a gold wreath.

B: SLOVENE FORCES, 1991
B1: *Major*, 31 Military Sub-District, Territorial Defence Force; Brnik Airport, June 1991
The Slovene TO tested greenish camouflage uniforms in 1989, approving browner camouflage field uniforms, service uniforms and insignia in Dec 1990 and issuing them from 24 May 1991. Most sleeve badges were issued after the Ten Day War; on the left upper sleeve the TO badge comprised a white-blue-red disc with three peaks, symbolizing the Triglav (the highest Slovene mountain), or – for 1991 Ig and Pekre conscripts – a '1' badge. On the right sleeve 1 Special Bde and the Guard of Honour Co wore unit badges. Command badges were worn on the left breast pocket fob of field uniforms and right pocket of service uniforms. On the camouflage mountain caps (green berets for special units), privates wore a Triglav on bronze crossed swords,

Rank insignia of Slovene Territorial Defence Force (TO), 24 May 1991–18 July 1993

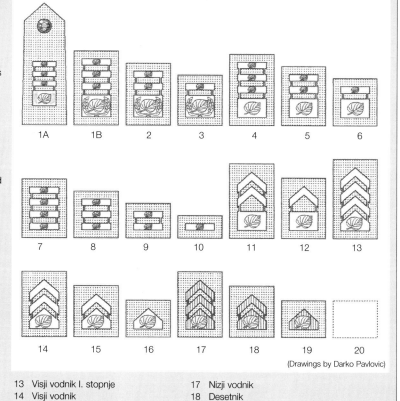

Metal insignia worn on uniform-colour shoulder straps of brown M91 officers' & NCOs' service tunic, greatcoat & light brown summer shirt; and on left breast pocket of all ranks' M91 camouflage jacket & shirt, and grey fatigue jacket.

General officers (1–3): 3–1 narrow gold bars with lime-leaves, over broad gold bar with wreathed lime-leaf.

Field officers (4–6): 3–1 narrow gold bars with lime-leaves over medium gold bar with lime-leaf.

Captains & subaltern officers (7–10): 4–1 narrow gold bars with lime-leaves.

Warrant & non-commissioned officers (11–16): 2–1 gold chevrons over medium gold bar with lime-leaf; 3–0 chevrons over gold pointed bar with lime-leaf.

Privates (17–20): 3–0 red chevrons over red pointed bar with gold lime-leaf; (20), no insignia.

Key to ranks:
1A Generalpolkovnik (shoulder strap)
1B Generalpolkovnik (breast)
2 Generalpodpolkovnik
3 Generalmajor
4 Polkovnik
5 Podpolkovnik
6 Major
7 Stotnik I. stopnje
8 Stotnik
9 Porocnik
10 Podporocnik
11 Zastavnik I. stopnje
12 Zastavnik
13 Visji vodnik I. stopnje
14 Visji vodnik
15 Vodnik I. stopnje
16 Vodnik
17 Nizji vodnik
18 Desetnik
19 Poddesetnik
20 Vojak

(Drawings by Darko Pavlovic)

Officers wore gold pips and bars embroidered in traditional *troplet* pattern, stitched to brown loops on the shoulder straps of brown M92 greatcoat, raincoat, ceremonial tunic, winter service tunic, light brown summer tunic & white shirt (A); from 1996, metal insignia on black shoulder straps (B), later black loops (C). NCOs wore pips and chevrons on both upper sleeves of these uniforms, with plain shoulder straps (D). The same insignia in gold embroidery were worn on dark brown patches, with gold inner edging, on the left breast pocket of all ranks' M91 green fatigue jacket, summer shirt, camouflage field jacket & shirt (E). (21), no insignia.

General officers (1–4): 4–1 pips over broad/narrow/broad bars.

Field officers (5–8): 4–1 pips over one narrow, one medium bars.

Captains & subaltern officers (9–12): 4–1 pips over narrow (later medium) bar.

Warrant & non-commissioned officers (13–18): 3–1 pips over one narrow, one broad chevrons; 3–1 pips over narrow chevron.

Privates (19–20): 2–1 pips on breast patch.

Key to ranks:

1	Stozerni general (20.6.1995 > only)	11	Porucnik
2	General zbora	12	Zastavnik
3	General pukovnik	13	Casnicki namjesnik
4	General bojnik	14	Stozerni narednik
5	Stozerni brigadir (20.6.1995 > only)	15	Narednik
		16	Stozerni vodnik (> 20.6.1995 only)
6	Brigadir	17	Vodnik
7	Pukovnik	18	Desetnik
8	Bojnik	19	Razvodnik
9	Satnik	20	Pozornik
10	Natporucnik	21	Gardist/ Vojnik

(Drawings by Darko Pavlovic)

officers and NCOs adding a lime leaf wreath (green for general officers). The service cap badge substituted gold for bronze.

B2: *Desetnik*, Brezice Company, 25 MSD, Territorial Defence Force; Medvedjek, July 1991

The Slovene TO had worn JNA uniforms since 1968, with the mountain cloak and cap – usually the 1950s pattern. In the late 1980s most units received the JNA M77 uniform and replaced the cloak with the winter coat. Only a few units had been issued the Slovene M90 uniform by June 1991, but all personnel wore the new cap badges. Units formed from JNA Partisan Brigades refused to wear their JNA sidecaps, pinning their new badges to the left breast pocket to identify themselves as Slovene TO.

B3: *Inspektor*, Slovene Police; Sentilj, July 1991

Slovene Police wore modified Yugoslav police uniforms, ranks and insignia agreed in 1986 and issued in March 1987, with special sleeve badges, black leather traffic police jackets and other items. The issue comprised a lead-blue peaked cap, mountain cap, tunic and trousers, dark blue summer and winter jackets and light blue shirts. A grey work uniform was introduced in the early 1980s, initially for the Slovene Special and Protection Police. Regular police and some reservists received new cap badges on 25 June 1991, replacing the JNA pattern with gold rays; those who did not get them simply wore no caps during the Ten Day War. The 'MILICA' title was worn on the left upper sleeve of all uniforms except the shirt. The MPC-1 helmet illustrated was manufactured by the Slovene company PAP in the second half of the 1980s and was also worn by other ex-Yugoslav police forces.

C: SERBIAN MILITIAS

C1: *Dobrovoljac*, Chetnik Detachments; Croatia, 1991

The SCP received JNA uniforms and equipment and commonly wore paratroopers' camouflage uniforms. The 'Volunteer' illustrated wears a traditional Serbian *sajkaca* cap with commercially bought wreathed double-headed eagle, a JNA 'tiger stripe' camouflage summer shirt, and JNA paratrooper leaf-pattern sleeveless smock and trousers. Militiamen, often bearded, had no rank insignia but did wear various sleeve badges, usually incorporating a skull-and-crossbones and other Chetnik and Royal Yugoslav insignia;

one of the first badges was a Serbian tricolour chevron with a cross and the four Cyrillic 'S' characters of the traditional Serbian motto – 'Only Unity will Save the Serbs'.

C2: *Pukovnik*, Serbian Volunteer Guard; Vukovar, November 1991

The SDG wore this green uniform or a camouflage uniform of unknown origin, black uniforms, or surplus US Army M82 camouflage, all with the SDG badge on the right upper sleeve, and on the left upper sleeve a tiger's head on a Serbian flag and 'TIGROVI' (Tigers). Green, black or red berets were worn, with either the Krajina TO rectangular Serbian flag badge, the Serbian and Krajina Police flag on a gold ornamental base, or a metal 'Tigers' badge. JNA breast badges indicated rank; Zeljko 'Arkan' Raznjatovic, who wore no rank insignia, promoted his men to officer rank and at least three to general officers – although only the SDG recognized the ranks; this man is ostensibly a colonel.

C3: *Dobrovoljac*, Serbian Guard; Gospic, September 1991

Operating without JNA logistic support, the anti-communist SG wore surplus US Army summer uniforms, with the SG title and quadruple Cyrillic 'S' badge on the left upper sleeve or above the left breast pocket. Personnel wore a silver eagle badge on a black beret, and no rank insignia.

D: CROATIAN FORCES, 1991
D1: *Vojnik*, 'Marko Kovac' Detachment, Territorial Defence Force; Cakovec, September 1991

The Croatian TO wore JNA uniforms and insignia until 1990, exchanging their *titovka* sidecaps for peaked mountain caps in 1991. The cap and sleeve badges or armbands incorporated the Croatian coat-of-arms, comprising a post-1945 Croatian red-and-white chequered straight-sided 'Spanish' shield *(sahovnica)* with a red top-left square, and a crest featuring the shields of Croatia's five historic provinces – Croatia proper, Dubrovnik, Dalmatia, Istria and Slavonia. This private wears a JNA M75 summer shirt and trousers, JNA conscripts' equipment, a cap with a curve-sided chequered shield, and a locally produced Croatian flag armband – in summer 1991 some personnel wore paper stickers as temporary identification. Rank insignia were rarely worn, to avoid confusion with the JNA. He carries a Slovene Gorenje MGV-176 sub-machine gun purchased by the local TO District.

D2: *Policajac specijalac*, 'Rakitje' Special Purpose Unit; Plitvice, March 1991

The pre-1990 Croatian Police Special Purpose Unit wore tiger-stripe camouflage uniforms, as did other Yugoslav Special Police and Krajina Police. When the SJP formed in Sept 1990 the original 1,800 members resorted to surplus US Army M82 winter camouflage uniforms. On the left upper sleeve they wore a white framed 'POLICIJA' title on a curved green backing. The Croatian Police had worn a framed 'MILICIJA' on a dark-blue backing since Dec 1977, also adopted in the second half of the 1980s by the Serbian Montenegrin, Vojvodina and Federal Special Police. The cap badge was the M90 Croatian curved 'baroque' chequered shield with gold rays, replaced in March 1991 by the M91

'crested baroque' chequered shield on silver rays in a gold wreath. Only a few senior officers wore rank insignia. This policeman carries an SAR-80 rifle, smuggled into Croatia in large numbers in 1990–91.

D3: *Policajac I. klase*, Dubrovnik Police Department; November 1991

The Croatian Police wore Croatian M86 uniforms with shoulder strap rank insignia; peaked caps with a red star badge, replaced in March 1991 by the M91 badge; raincoats, and tiger-stripe camouflage field uniforms. Following rapid police expansion several thousand Slovene Police grey work uniforms were purchased in late 1990, and subsequently manufactured as the standard work uniform. The uniform comprised a jacket with four flapped pockets, trousers with two side pockets and two flapped thigh pockets, berets, and JNA officers' boots and belts. A white framed 'POLICIJA' title on a grey backing was worn on the left upper sleeve; sleeve shields introduced in July 1991 were often sewn beneath this. Croatian Police cap badges were initially a red star on gold rays, partly replaced in summer 1990 by the Police 1st pattern M90 uncrested 'Spanish' chequered shield with scalloped top; removed in Aug 1990 to avoid further antagonizing the Krajina Serbs, this was replaced in late 1990 by the Police 2nd pattern M90 Croatian 'uncrested baroque' chequered shield with gold rays; and in 1991 by the Police M91 'crested baroque' shield with silver rays in a gold wreath. The grey work beret had either no badge, or the Police 2nd pattern M90 or M91 badges. Rank insignia were not prescribed, but this senior constable is unofficially wearing his raincoat rank insignia: yellow chevrons piped light blue, on a dark blue backing.

E: CROATIAN FORCES, 1991
E1: Officer, 106th Brigade, National Guard Corps; Osijek, September 1991

Initially the ZNG wore JNA M77, Slovene Police grey work, or US Army M82 camouflage uniforms; but locally produced camouflage uniforms were soon introduced – the tiger-stripe or leaf 'Police pattern' illustrated, or more usually a close copy of the US M82. As Ministry of Internal Affairs personnel, often commanded by regular Police officers, ZNG senior officers sometimes wore their Police shoulder strap rank insignia, but lower ranks wore no insignia until the ZNG became the Croatian Army in Oct 1991. Personnel wore the ZNG M91 cap badge, comprising a 'crested baroque' chequered shield in a gold *troplet* wreath, or TO or Croatian Police badges. The ZNG badge on the upper left sleeve showed the cap badge above black crossed rifles, above 'ZNG RH' (*Zbor narodne garde Republike Hrvatske* – National Guard Corps of the Republic of Croatia).

E2: *Vojnik*, 129th Brigade, Croatian Army; Karlovac, December 1991

During the huge expansion of Oct–Nov 1991 the HV purchased thousands of surplus East German Army M56/76 helmets, and M90 winter uniforms in 'rain'-pattern camouflage, with shoulder straps removed and the ZNG pattern sleeve badge with 'HV' initials added. Initially only generals wore breast rank insignia, and when lower ranks were issued them in the second half of 1992 the East German uniforms had mostly worn out. Croatian forces

Rank insignia of Slovene, Croatian & Krajina Police

(Note: Insignia used by **Slovene Police** to February 1992; **Croatian Police** to 25 July 1991 officially, actually seen until January 1992; & **Krajina Police** 1991–96.)

All ranks of Slovene, Croatian & Krajina Police were still wearing M86 Yugoslav shoulder strap insignia with local variations in ranks. Shoulder straps were dark blue or dark grey. Krajina insignia introduced 22 June 1993 had no blue piping, but 20mm braid bars and 10mm & 20mm chevrons set at a 90° angle.

Interior Ministry officials (1–4): 4–1 gold embroidered stars over 3x 16mm gold braid bars; gold piping.

Regional Secretariat officials – Krajina (5–6): 2–1 gold embroidered stars over 1x 10mm & 2x 20mm gold braid bars; gold piping.

Senior officers (7–10): 4–1 gold embroidered stars over 2x 16mm gold braid bars; gold piping.

Junior officers (11, 12, 14): 3–1 gold embroidered stars over 16mm gold braid bar.

Probationary officers (13, 15): 2–1 white embroidered stars over 16mm white braid bar; no piping.

Constables (16–21): 1–0 gold embroidered stars over 3–1x 10mm, and 2 –0x 16mm gold braid chevrons.

Cadets (22–24): 1 x 10mm or 16mm white braid bar or chevron; no piping.

Key to ranks:
Slovene Police (S) & Croatian Police (C), ranks as at 25 June 1991; Krajina Police (K), ranks as at 22 June 1993. (Translations in parentheses.)

1. **(S)** Ministar za notranje zadeve; **(C)** Ministar unutarnjih poslova; **(K)** Ministar Ministarstva unutrasnih poslova (Interior Minister)
2. **(S)** Namestnik ministra za notranje zadeve; **(C)** Zamjenik ministra unutarnjih poslova; **(K)** Zamjenik ministra Ministarstva unutrasnjih poslova (Deputy Interior Minister)
3. **(S)** Poveljnik milice (Police Commander); **(C)** Podsekretar u Ministarstvu unutarnjih poslova (Interior Ministry Undersecretary); **(K)** Pomocnik ministra Ministarstva unutrasnjih poslova (Assistant Interior Minister)
4. **(S)** Glavni inspektor I. razreda (Principal Inspector 1st Class); **(C)** Pomocnik ministra unutarnjih poslova (Assistant Interior Minister)
5. **(K)** Sekretar sekretarijata unutrasnjih poslova (Regional Interior Secretary)
6. **(K)** Zamjenik sekretara sekretarijata unutrasnjih poslova (Deputy Regional Interior Secretary)¶
7. **(S, C & K)** Glavni inspektor (Principal Inspector)
8. **(S)** Visji inspektor I. razreda; **(C & K)** Visi inspektor I. klase (Chief Inspector 1st Class)
9. **(S)** Visji inspektor; **(C & K)** Visi inspektor (Chief Inspector)
10. **(S)** Samostojni inspektor; **(C & K)** Samostalni inspektor (Independent Inspector)
11. **(S)** Inspektor I. razreda; **(C & K)** Inspektor I. klase (Inspector 1st Class)
12. **(S, C & K)** Inspektor (Inspector)
13. **(C & K)** Pripravnik inspektor (Probationary Inspector)
14. **(S)** Nizji inspektor; **(C & K)** Mladji inspektor (Junior Inspector)
15. **(C & K)** Pripravnik mladji inspektor (Probationary Junior Inspector)
16. **(S)** Samostojni milicnik; **(C & K)** Visi milicionar (Master Constable)
17. **(S)** Visji milicnik I. razreda; **(C & K)** Stariji milicionar I. klase (Senior Constable 1st Class)
18. **(S)** Visji milicnik; **(C & K)** Stariji milicionar (Senior Constable)
19. **(S)** Milicnik I. razreda; **(C & K)** Milicionar I. klase (Constable 1st Class)
20. **(S)** Milicnik; **(C & K)** Milicionar (Constable)
21. **(S)** Nizji milicnik; **(C & K)** Mladji milicionar (Junior Constable)
22. **(S)** Pripravnik za milicnika; **(C & K)** Pripravnik mladji milicionar (Probationary Junior Constable)
23. **(C)** Student Fakulteta kriminalistiekih znanosti (Police College Student)
24. **(S)** Ucenec kadetske sole za milicnike; **(C)** Polaznik srednje skole za unutarnje poslove (Police Cadet)

(Drawings by Darko Pavlovic)

also wore other camouflage uniforms, including the ,British M84 and West German M90; and a wide variety of helmets, predominantly the US M1, but also the Swiss M49/62 (a copy of the British AT Mk II), British Mk IV, the Polish version of the Soviet Ssh40, Yugoslav M59/85, and Slovene MPC-1.

E3: Officer, HOS Militia; Vukovar, October 1991

The HOS wore US Army M82 camouflage uniforms in winter and summer leaf-pattern as combat uniform, with black berets or Croatian peaked fieldcaps; and locally produced US Army uniforms in black as everyday uniform with red

Special Police officials, Special Police Units (SJP), Lucko Counter-Terrorist Police Unit (ATJ) and Air Units wore embroidered six-point stars or diamonds on green-brown rectangular patches with *troplet* pattern edging and bars. Insignia introduced in 1992 but only generally distributed after official introduction on 13 May 1995 (although Asst Min Josko Moric and SJP Chief Mladen Markac were photographed wearing badges 3 & 4 respectively before 1995).

Interior Ministry officials (1–4): 4–1 yellow embroidered stars with double *troplet* edging, (4) single edging & bar, on 8cm x 5cm patch.

Special Police officers (5–8): 4–1 yellow embroidered stars with single *troplet* edging & bar, or plain edging, on 8cm x 4cm (5), or 7cm x 4cm (6–8) patch.

Special Police Constables (9–11): 3–1 yellow embroidered diamonds edged black, on 7cm x 4cm patch edged black.

Probationary Special Police Constable (12): White embroidered diamond edged black on 7cm x 4cm patch edged black.

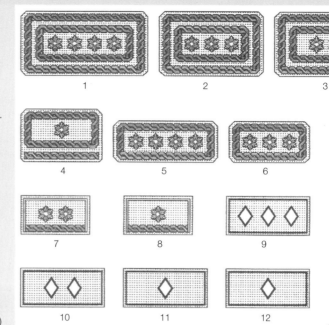

(Drawings by Darko Pavlovic)

Key to ranks (with translations):
1. Ministar unutarnjih poslova (Interior Minister)
2. Zamjenik ministra UP (Deputy Int Min)
3. Pomocnik ministra UP nadlezan za poslove specijalne policije (Asst Int Min for Special Police)
4. Nacelnik sektora SP (SP Sector Chief)
5. Nacelnik odjela SP (SP Department Chief; also Commanders of Lucko ATJ & Air Unit)
6. Zapovjednik specijalne jedinice policijske uprave (SJP Cdr, also Deputy ATJ Cdr, & Senior Pilot)
7. Pomocnik zapovjednika u SJPU (Asst SJP Cdr; also Asst ATJ Cdr, & 1st Class Pilot)
8. Instruktor specijalisticke obuke u SJPU (SJP Specialist Instructor; also Spec ATJ Instr, & 2nd–5th Class Pilot)
9. Vodja specijalisticke skupine u SJPU (SJP Spec Group Leader; also Spec ATJ Gp Ldr, & Flight Technician)
10. Zamjenik vodje specijalisticke skupine u SJPU (SJP Dpty Spec Gp Ldr; also Dpty Spec ATJ Gp Ldr, & Air Technician)
11. Policajac specijalac u SJPU (SJP & ATJ Constable
12. Policajac specijalac–vjezbenik u SJPU (SJP & ATJ Probationary Constable, also Prob Air Tech)

berets – although shortages meant that both types might be worn in either capacity. The cap and beret badge was a pre-1945 Croatian coat-of-arms, comprising an uncrested chequered 'Spanish' shield with a white top-left square. Dating from the Middle Ages until May 1945, this is misleadingly identified with the World War II Ustasha government. The round sleeve badge betrayed the HOS's Ustasha sympathies, showing a pre-1945 chequered square in an Ustasha-style *troplet* ring, with 'HOS' above 'HSP', above the Ustasha greeting 'ZA DOM SPREMNI' – roughly, 'We are ready to defend the homeland'. Personnel wore HV breast rank insignia, and sometimes replicas of Ustasha officers' cap badges and other NDH insignia on their berets or breast pockets; they were ordered to remove these on transfer to the HV in December 1991.

F: SERBIAN KRAJINA FORCES, 1991–95
F1: *Vodnik*, Krajina Territorial Defence Force, 1991
The Krajina TO used JNA uniforms, equipment and weapons; by the end of 1991 most troops had tiger-stripe camouflage similar to that used by the JNA Military Police and Special Forces, or various Yugoslav Special Police uniforms but with some differences in cut. Due to wartime shortages the Krajina TO and SVK subsequently introduced more Yugoslav or Srpska Republic uniforms, and leaf-pattern camouflage gradually replaced the tiger-stripe. All Krajina units wore berets with JNA red star badges, or later metal rectangular Serbian flags. JNA breast rank insignia were worn and some units had sleeve insignia, but there was no general Krajina TO sleeve badge.

F2: *Brigadni djeneral*, Serbian Krajina Army, 1993
On formation in late 1992 the SVK wore a variety of mostly JNA camouflage uniforms, predominantly leaf-pattern. This brigadier general wears a standard JNA camouflage summer shirt with JNA breast rank insignia, trousers, belt and boots. On the right upper sleeve is the SVK badge, representing the Serbian coat of arms on a white crowned two-headed eagle with swords in its claws and 'SVK' in Cyrillic script; this was also worn, without the title, as an oval cloth beret badge, although the Krajina Police badge was also worn.

F3: *Stariji milicionar*, Krajina Police Field Force, 1994
The Krajina Police wore obsolete Croatian Police M77 and M86 blue uniforms, JNA Air Force and paratrooper blue uniforms, JNA tiger-stripe and leaf-pattern camouflage, or Serbian Police blue tiger-stripe and leaf-patterns. This senior

constable wears a Serbian Police summer shirt and trousers. Initially Croatian Police rank insignia were worn, but the 22 June 1993 regulations added two senior ranks and abolished the light blue shoulder strap piping. The cap badge is a M92 metal Serbian tricolour on a gold ornamental base. The Serbian blue camouflage uniforms usually came with a white framed cyrillic 'MILICIJA' title on a curved blue backing on both upper sleeves, but this policeman wears on the left sleeve an armband with a semi-circular badge depicting the Serbian tricolour flag and 'MILICIJA KRAJINA', as introduced in early 1991.

G: CROATIAN FORCES, 1991–95
G1: *Pripadnik*, People's Defence Force, October 1991
The NZ combined any available military and police camouflage uniform items with civilian clothing. This member wears a locally made US Army-type field cap in a yellowish camouflage, a matching winter jacket with pocket snap-fasteners, blue jeans, no webbing and black JNA boots. He has stitched on the upper half of a ZNG or HV sleeve badge as a makeshift cap badge; various official ZNG, TO or Police badges were also worn. The round sleeve badge had the inscription 'NARODNA ZASTITA' above a red-white-blue Croatian flag with clasped bare and armoured hands, above two swords forming a peak. NZ units were usually issued obsolete weapons; this man has an old Yugoslav M48 rifle.

G2: *General-pukovnik*, Croatian Army, 1993
An experimental officers' and NCOs' service uniform was introduced on 15 Jan 1992 for President Tudjman's aides and the Guard of Honour unit, and was generally issued from 27 Nov 1992. It comprised a brown peaked cap, tunic, trousers and greatcoat, a light brown summer shirt, black shoes and equipment; later a lighter brown-grey lightweight summer uniform was added. Officers wore embroidered rank insignia on both cuffs of the experimental tunic, but from Nov 1992 yellow thread insignia on brown cloth shoulder straps, from 1996 gilt insignia on black shoulder straps and later black shoulder slides. NCOs wore sleeve rank insignia. The gilt cap badge was a crested Croatian coat-of-arms on a V-shaped *troplet* chevron, superimposed on crossed swords in an oak-leaf wreath. General officers wore square brown collar patches piped gold, with a *troplet* pattern edging and gold embroidered 'HV' initials; other officers and NCOs had gilt metal initials. No branch-of-service badges were worn. Air Force personnel wore silver insignia on dark blue uniforms; Navy officers gold cuff rings, and petty officers sleeve chevrons.

G3: *Vodnik*, Military Police Counter-Terrorist Unit, 1994
The ZNG Police *(Policija Zbora narodne garde)* was formed in July 1991, wearing locally produced sleeve unit badges and any available white webbing as their mark of status, while some units wore helmets marked with 'P', sometimes with two white bands. In Jan 1992 the Croatian Army Military Police *(Vojna policija – VP)* wore Croatian Police-style badges of office on black leather fobs on the left breast pocket, and, later that year, white webbing and the unit badge on a white brassard on the right shoulder. MP Counter-Terrorist Units (ATVP) were created in Jan 1993, personnel wearing a falcon's head motif as beret and arm badges. From Feb 1994 all Military Police wore a stylized falcon with outspread wings on the beret, brassard and left breast pocket fob, and a special 'VP' left upper sleeve badge. The ATVP received the new green overalls illustrated as camouflage in the field.

H: CROATIAN FORCES, 1995
H1: *Narednik*, 121st Home Defence Regiment; Nova Gradiska, May 1995
By 1995 the Croatian Army was well equipped, most personnel wearing Croatian camouflage uniforms modelled on the US Army M82 pattern. This senior sergeant wears a winter camouflage uniform with chest webbing and a Croatian M93 Sestan-Busch BK-3 helmet, based on the US M78 Kevlar model. On the left upper sleeve Home Defence units wore a crested coat-of-arms, above gold crossed rifles, above the initials 'HV', within a *troplet* oval above the gold title 'DOMOBRANSTVO'. This NCO wears his rank insignia on the chest webbing – an unusual practice, especially in combat. Rank titles and insignia were officially introduced on 1 Nov 1991, with the first appointments on 4 Dec 1991, but NCOs did not receive insignia until mid 1992. Command and speciality badges were introduced in Feb 1992.

H2: *Bojnik*, 7th Guards Brigade; Knin, August 1995
Initially the seven élite Guards brigades wore US Army M82 camouflage uniforms, but by 1995 most used Croatian patterns. This major wears a Croatian summer camouflage uniform, with a parachute qualification badge above the right breast pocket (there were three variants – metal, cloth and subdued). Guards brigades wore metal unit beret badges repeated as an embroidered badge on the right upper sleeve, and left upper sleeve badges incorporating the brigade title: 1 Gds Bde = black beret with gilt tiger's head; 2 Gds Bde = dark green beret with silver lightning in a fist on a shield; 3 Gds Bde = black beret with gilt marten; 4 Gds Bde = red beret with silver lions and swords; 5 Gds Bde = black beret with gilt falcon; 7 Gds Bde = orange-brown beret with gilt puma's head; 9 Gds Bde = black beret with silver wolf's head.

H3: *Zapovjednik*, Zadar-Knin Special Police Unit, August 1995
In mid 1992 new green SJP uniforms were introduced, although other patterns were retained – leaf-pattern camouflage; white, or white with splotches of brown and grey, for snow conditions; and black for counter-terrorist operations. A round brown version of the blue Croatian Police shield was worn on the left upper sleeve, and an arrowhead badge (inspired by that of the US Army Special Forces) on the right upper sleeve (see photograph on page 49). SJP rank insignia, worn above the left breast pocket, appeared in 1992 and were officially issued on 24 Apr 1995. SJP reservists did not wear rank insignia or the arrowhead badge. Personnel wore a yellow unit title above the right breast pocket, and a few units wore unit badges on the upper sleeve, breast pocket or field cap. The service uniform introduced later comprised a green peaked cap, tunic and trousers, with shoulder strap rank insignia, white shirt and black tie.

INDEX